CREATING INTERACTIVE ENVIRONMENTS IN THE SECONDARY SCHOOL

CREATING INTERACTIVE ENVIRONMENTS

IN THE SECONDARY SCHOOL

Lois T. Stover

Gloria A. Neubert

James C. Lawlor

INTERACTIVE
RESOURCES
S E R I E S

An NEA Professional Library Publication

NATIONAL EDUCATION ASSOCIATION

Washington, D.C.

Library of Congress Cataloging-in-Publication Data

Stover, Lois T.
    Creating interactive environments in the secondary school /by Lois T. Stover,
Gloria A. Neubert, James C. Lawlor.
        p. cm. — (Interactive resources)
    Includes bibliographical references.
    ISBN 0-8106-3351-5
    1. Active learning—United States.   2. Education, Secondary—United States.
3. Classroom environment—United States.   4. Interaction analysis on education—United States.
I. Neubert, Gloria A.   II. Lawlor, James C.   III. Title.   IV. Series.
370.15'23—dc   93-19041
                                                                                                        CIP

Contents

Acknowledgments

THE AUTHORS

Lois T. Stover is Associate Professor of Secondary Education at Towson State University, Towson, Maryland.

Gloria A. Neubert is Professor of Secondary Education at Towson State University, Towson, Maryland. She is also the author of *Inductive Reasoning in the Secondary Classroom*.

James C. Lawlor is Professor of Secondary Education at Towson State University, Towson, Maryland.

NOTE:

The opinions expressed in this publication should not be construed as representing the policy or position of the National Education Association. Materials published by the NEA Professional Library are intended to be discussion documents for educators who are concerned with specialized interests of the profession.

ADVISORY PANEL

Georgia Lee Eshelman
Social Studies Teacher
Lehman Junior High School
Canton, Ohio

Janice S. Fitzgerald
Executive Deputy
Office of the Chancellor
Pennsylvania State System of
    Higher Education
Harrisburg, Pennsylvania

Donna Grzybowski
Social Studies Teacher
Anna L. Klein School
Guttenberg, New Jersey

J. Merrell Hansen
Associate Professor of
    Education
Brigham Young University
Provo, Utah

John Moffitt
Chairman of Mathematics
Windham High School
Windham, Maine

Perry Ross
Principal
Mediapolis Community
    Schools
Sperry, Iowa

John J. Tzeng
Professor Emeritus
Education and Technology
University of the District of
    Columbia
Washington, D.C.

Judith Winzenz
Department Chair, Teacher
    of English
Appleton East High School
Appleton, Wisconsin

Kathleen D. Yothers
Department Head
Chairperson
Health and Physical
    Education
Franklin Regional School
    District
Murrysville, Pennsylvania

INTRODUCTION

Recent national studies of education (e.g., Goodlad 1984, Astin 1985, Smith 1986, Lounsbury 1991) have expressed a desperate need for teachers to move beyond their traditional authoritarian function as the primary source of knowledge in the classroom. These studies call for teachers to develop lessons in which students become more active and responsible learners and less passive recipients of someone else's knowledge.

This call for classrooms to be places in which teachers and students collaborate in the teaching-learning process has its historical foundations in the work of many prominent educational leaders. For example, Socrates viewed teaching as a "cooperative art" between teacher and students, and John Dewey characterized the teacher as an intellectual guide, rather than as a presenter of abstract knowledge passively absorbed by students. More recently, educational theorists and researchers (e.g., Vygotsky 1978, Smith 1986, Adler and Towne 1987) have encouraged practitioners to view learning as a process whereby learners construct knowledge through active cognitive involvement. Such cognitive involvement requires a classroom environment that is interactive, in other words, a place where students maximize the use of their listening, speaking, reading, and writing skills in order to interact with their teachers; their peers; and with visual, auditory, and tactile materials.

The purpose of this text is to instruct you, the readers—preservice and inservice teachers—about the need to establish such interactive classrooms and to provide guidance to you as you seek to implement a more interactive pedagogy. However, unlike many other texts written about pedagogy, this text is not intended to simply transmit knowledge about interactive instruction. It is designed to involve you actively so that you will construct knowledge as you read, and thus ultimately be able to prepare your own interactive lessons.

CHAPTER STRUCTURE

In order to facilitate this process, each chapter begins with Readiness, a section that asks you to recall experience pertinent to what you are about to learn. Its purpose is to mobilize your background so that you can relate the new information to what you already know—a necessary step if new information is to be meaningful to you, the learner, and teacher.

Within the Readiness section are purpose-for-reading questions to answer while you read. These questions will help you focus attention on the information in the chapter and will keep you actively involved, processing the information as you search for the answers. More specific questions and activities, which require you to reflect (sometimes in writing), are also included throughout the chapters to continue to prod your active cognitive engagement with the information.

At the end of the chapters, you will find a series of Practice activities designed to give you opportunities to design interactive strategies for your own content. Sometimes these activities encourage you to interact with a partner—another student in your workshop or class or a colleague in your school—in order to facilitate and affirm your learning.

The Practice sections are followed by Classroom Carry-Over sections that ask you to write down ways you can carry over newly acquired information about interactive learning into your very own classroom.

CHAPTER CONTENT

The information in each chapter follows a basic instructional progression as well.

Chapter 1, Passive vs. Interactive Environments, develops the concept of an "interactive environment" through the use of an exemplar lesson and a contrasting nonexample.

Chapter 2, The Value of Interactive Instruction, provides, in a reader-friendly manner, the research and theory that undergirds this approach to teaching. This chapter is designed to assist teachers in understanding the "why" of interactive instruction so that they can select appropriate teaching strategies and explain or defend their choices.

Chapters 3, 4, 5, and 6 are on listening, speaking, reading, and writing, respectively, as they are used in interactive, secondary classrooms from art to zoology. Each of these chapters presents a myriad of teaching strategies and lesson approaches that require students to capitalize on their listening, speaking, reading, and writing skills in order to interact with peers, teachers, and instructional materials.

Chapter 7, Instruction Planners, provides a one-page guide for each of the language-processing skills covered in this book. You can use these guides to check your thinking as you design lessons. For example, if you are planning a lesson in which students must listen actively, you can turn to the page entitled "When My Students Are Listening in this Lesson, Have I . . . ?"for guidance. When you plan lessons that require students to read text, you can refer to the one-page guide entitled "If My Students Are Reading

in this Lesson, Have I . . . ?" If you want students to speak during a class session, the page "When My Students Are Speaking in this Lesson, Have I . . . ?" will prove useful. And you can think about ways to involve students in lessons through writing-to-learn strategies by reviewing the questions on the page, "Could My Students Write in this Lesson in Order to . . . ?"

LEARNING-STYLE ADJUSTMENTS

One final point about this text should be kept in mind as you read it. Different readers have different learning styles, as do the students you find in the classroom. Thus, you may find that doing the writing activities embedded throughout the text, especially in the writing chapter, feels cumbersome if you are a strongly extroverted person who prefers speaking to writing. On the other hand, if you are more introspective, you may find the writing activities very comfortable, while you respond less enthusiastically to participating in speaking activities. That's why we have presented a variety of activities in each chapter. As a teacher, you will have to pick and choose those strategies best suited to

you and your students. At the same time, we hope that after having experienced, yourself, the various strategies described in this interactive text, you will appreciate that all students, no matter what their preferred learning style, need to develop all of their language-processing faculties. Thus, they should be guided through activities that promote their listening, speaking, reading, and writing abilities and which, at the same time, help them become more interactive, responsible partners in the teaching-learning process.

BIBLIOGRAPHY

- Adler, R. B. and Towne, N. *Looking Out/Looking In*. Fifth edition. New York: Holt, Rinehart, and Winston, 1987.
- Astin, A.W. 1985. *Achieving Educational Excellence*. San Francisco: Jossey-Bass.
- Goodlad, J.I. 1984. *A Place Called School*. New York: McGraw-Hill
- Lounsbury, J.H. 1991. *Inside Grade Eight: From Apathy to Excitement*. Washington, D.C.: National Association of Secondary School Principals.
- NIE Study Group. 1984. *Involvement in Learning*. Washington, D.C.: NIE.
- Smith, F. 1986. *Insult to Intelligence*. Portsmith, N.H.: Heinemann.
- Vygotsky, L.S. 1978. *Mind in Society: The Development of Higher Psychological Processes*. Cambridge, Mass.: Harvard University Press.

Passive vs. Interactive Environments

What types of activities do you use to actively engage students in learning?

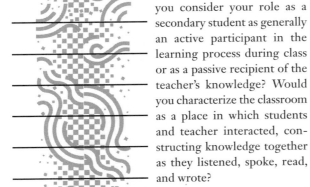

READINESS

Recall your secondary school education. Imagine the classes you attended. What types of activities do you remember as typical in your classes? Did the teachers engage you in class discussions? Did you participate in small groups for discussion? Did you listen to lectures? Did you participate in role-playing activities? When you read in your classes, did you discuss the reading? Did you write about the reading? Did you write in classes other than English and for purposes other than testing? What type of writing did you do? Would you consider your role as a secondary student as generally an active participant in the learning process during class or as a passive recipient of the teacher's knowledge? Would you characterize the classroom as a place in which students and teacher interacted, constructing knowledge together as they listened, spoke, read, and wrote?

Purpose for Reading

Two lesson descriptions follow. Both lessons are designed to enable secondary students to list the major events that led to the initiation of the Revolutionary War and to articulate reasons proposed by colonists for remaining under the jurisdiction of the British Crown and for separating from it. The reading material in this chapter will help you answer these questions: In which lesson are the students more active participants in the learning process? In which lesson are the students more involved in constructing knowledge as they interact with the teacher, each other, and text by using all of their language-processing facilities?

READING MATERIAL

Read the following two lesson plans.

Lesson 1

Ms. Jones takes attendance as her eighth grade U.S. history students settle into their seats. She reads the objectives already on the chalkboard, saying, "Today you will learn the reasons why some colonists began to want independence from Britain and reasons why others continued to lobby for maintaining the existing relationship between the colonies and the Crown." Ms. Jones then begins the lesson by asking students to list and explain specific key events, including events such as the passage of the Navigation Acts; the Stamp Act of 1765; and then the Intolerable Acts of 1774, which affected the colonists' perceptions of their relationship to England. Ms. Jones leads the students through a chronological listing of these events, which they recall from the chapter entitled "The Road Toward Independence" that they were supposed to read for homework. She asks for students to volunteer information about the various acts; after a student has contributed a response, she uses the overhead projector to show the class what key points they should copy into their notes.

After ensuring that the class has the list of major events written down, Ms. Jones then continues with a lecture that she organizes by using a chart with the two columns "Reasons Against Separating" and "Reasons for Separating," filling it in as she talks. She has passed out to the students a blank chart (Figure 1.1) that the students use to organize their note taking.

As her class time draws to a close, Ms. Jones tells the students, "Now you should be able to list the key events that led many colonists to begin to think about independence from Britain." She goes on to tell her class to read the chapter in their text entitled "The

Figure 1.1

Ms. Jones's Chart

Reasons for Separating	Reasons Against Separating
1. Desire for economic independence	1. Desire for military protection
2. _____	2. _____
3. _____	3. _____

Shot Heard 'Round the World," which is about the battle of Lexington and Concord, in preparation for class the next day.

Lesson 2

Mr. Smith has the following instructions written on the board for his eighth grade U.S. history students to follow as they enter the room: "Open your notebooks and write freely for three minutes about how you, as an eighth grader, are both dependent on and independent of your parents or the adults with whom you live. Also, imagine how you will respond to this same topic when you are 18 and about to graduate from high school." After he takes attendance, he tells students to wrap up what they are writing, and he calls on several students to share their written responses. As they talk, he makes lists on the board of ways in which the students imagine they will be both independent of and yet still dependent on adults when they are older. For instance, some students say they are currently more independent than they used to be because they now baby-sit and mow lawns and so have money of their own to spend; however, they are still dependent on their parents for major expenses, but after high school graduation, they will have to take more responsibility for their economic security. Other students discuss how, at age 13, they have limited freedom of movement and must depend on parents to take them places unless they can walk or ride a bike, but note that, after age 16, they will be more mobile—although they may not be able to afford a car of their own, they will be able to drive.

Next Mr. Smith asks, "We've been studying the colonial period. What does asking you to write about your relationship to adults now and at 18 have to do with the colonies and their relationship to England?" After several students have contributed answers, such as noting that the colonies, like the students themselves, are developing increased skill and ability to take care of themselves over time, he tells students to open their texts to the chapter entitled "The Road Toward Independence." He instructs the students to take 10 minutes to skim the reading, looking for key incidents that affected the colonists' perceptions about their relationship with Britain, which eventually contributed to the start of the Revolution.

After Mr. Smith calls time, he tells the students to move into pairs based on classroom proximity. Each pair is to create a chart, based on what they have just read, which indicates key events and their dates in one column, and the resulting effects on colonial/Crown relations in the other column. After 10 minutes, he calls on different pairs to contribute events to a master chart, and the class as a whole helps to organize the events in sequential order and to clarify the significance of each item listed.

Mr. Smith now tells the students to get out of their seats. He tells some students to imagine they are merchants in the colonial times, others to imagine being farmers, others to imagine they work for the colonial government, others to imagine they are trappers, and so on. Given their role, students are to move to the left of the classroom if they would have voted for independence at the time of the Intolerable Acts; they should move to the right of the room if they would still opt for the existing relationship with Britain. The two groups of students now create lists of the reasons for their positions. After another 10 minutes, the groups present their arguments to each other, and each group has an opportunity to shape a rebuttal to the arguments offered by the other side.

Mr. Smith sends the students back to their seats and tells them to take three minutes to organize their notes for the day by using the points made in their discussion. He then asks them to swap what they have written with someone sitting nearby and then swap back and revise or add to their own notes as they deem necessary. He then asks students to volunteer to fill in the blank in the statement, "By the end of class today, we were able to _____." As he receives answers, he writes them on the board and asks students if they agree, shaping this statement of the objective until they reach consensus. For example, the students might complete the sentence by saying, "By the end of class today, we were able to discuss what effect those events had on the reasons the colonists articulated for remaining under the jurisdiction of the British Crown or for separating from it."

As the class period nears the end, Mr. Smith asks the class as a whole, "Those of you who were not yet for independence, what additional events or British actions would have to occur in order to sway you toward a position of valuing independence? Those of you who already want to achieve independence, what would you do now to move toward that goal?" Students respond, and he tells them to check their predictions as they read their assigned homework chapter, entitled "The Shot Heard 'Round the World." Additionally, he tells them that after they have finished reading, they should write, in their own words, a description of the first event in the Revolution.

Comparing Lessons

In which of the preceding lessons are students more actively involved in the learning process? In number two, Mr. Smith's lesson, of course. In fact, Mr. Smith's lesson provides students many opportunities for involvement in learning. They become actively involved in discovering an emotional connection between their own lives and the situation of the colonists just prior to the start of the Revolution. They become actively involved in extending their content knowledge and constructing a sense of an historical period through using their knowledge during the class session. The activities that Mr. Smith planned for them ensured this. His classroom is an example of an *interactive classroom environment*. He has planned

- instruction that requires students to listen and read as well as to talk and write in order to learn the content information, thereby engaging them in active cognitive processing (thinking) during their initial exposure to new information (see Figure 1.2),
- instruction that makes the students as cognitively active as their teacher, and
- instruction that makes initial exposure to the new content information simultaneous with learning the new content information.

Ms. Jones's lesson provides no opportunities for students

to *construct* knowledge for themselves. The students are passive recipients of Ms. Jones' knowledge, which she passed on to them by using an expository teaching method, the lecture. In fact, this lesson provides no guarantee that the students were cognitively engaged in the subject at all. Even when students answered questions for Ms. Jones, they merely reiterated what they had read, passing on the author's knowledge. Ms. Jones's classroom is an example of a *passive learning environment*. She has planned

- instruction that often mandates that students passively listen and read without a clear purpose (see Figure 1.2),
- instruction that puts students in the role of passive recipients of content information presented to them in final form,
- instruction that typically has the teacher more cognitively involved than the students, and
- instruction that provides no guarantee that initial exposure to the new information is simultaneous with student learning of that information.

IDENTIFICATION/ ANALYSIS

Go back to Mr. Smith's interactive lesson and make a list of the activities that engaged students directly in the learning. Compare your analysis to the analysis that follows.

The *first* activity designed to help students interact with the material, and that also

Interactive Environment	Passive Environment
Students	Students
• listen actively (with a stated purpose to draw their own conclusions),	• listen passively (with no stated purpose other than to record information),
• speak/talk to construct,	• speak/talk directly to the teacher and reiterate factual material,
• read actively (with a stated purpose),	• read with no stated purpose,
• write actively (to tap experience and construct knowledge),	• write without cognitive engagement (transcribe what the teacher says for the purpose of remembering her points as they were delivered to them),
• engage in independent thinking to construct knowledge.	• engage in dependent thinking to absorb someone else's construction of knowledge.

Figure 1.2
Classroom Environment

forms the basis of the lesson, occurs at the opening of the class session when Mr. Smith tells the students to *write* freely about ways they are dependent on and independent of their parents and adults at the present time and to predict how they will feel when they are approaching graduation from high school. Students then share their written responses orally; these ideas are listed on the chalkboard. Finally, Mr. Smith asks students how their dependence on and independence of adults relates to the ways in which the colonists interact with Great Britain, thereby establishing a connection between students'

lives and the topic under study. Mr. Smith is aware that one requirement for learning is the linking of new information with information already in the students' backgrounds, so he uses this brief writing activity to activate their thinking. The writing ensures active cognitive processing on the part of the students because in order to write, the students must think. The writing also serves to motivate the students by making the new learning relevant to their lives, a connection that they determine for themselves.

In contrast, Ms. Jones *tells* her students the objectives for the lesson, guaranteeing that *she* knows the purpose for the class session, but not guaranteeing that *students* are attending to it.

The *second activity* in Mr. Smith's lesson designed to help students interact with the material is the assignment to skim *read* the text chapter for the stated purpose of identifying key events (and dates) that led to the start of the Revolution. Students work briefly in pairs to create a chart, so that through their collaborative *talk*, they reinforce and check each others' understanding of

their reading, an understanding that they capture in *writing*. Mr. Smith then builds a master chart on the chalkboard, based on students' contributions. Students are active in the class at this point, either as speakers or listeners. As class members *listen* to their peers suggest events to be included on the master chart, they have, as a purpose for listening, the task of verifying the accuracy of the information offered. Disagreements result in further *talking* in order to reach final agreement on the content of the chart. Here, with the aid of the text, Mr. Smith has students actively involved in discovering content knowledge for themselves. They are engaged in active cognitive processing (thinking) during their initial exposure to new information because they have to determine which events are "key" events. With teacher guidance, students read, talk, and write to construct for themselves a chart reflecting their consensus about significant factors leading to a decision to move toward independence.

Ms. Jones, on the other hand, asks students to explain the significance of key events that she has already determined to be important and has already listed on the overhead. She shapes students' responses to fit information *she* wants to record. She provides them with a chart to guide their note taking and to ensure that they note *her* explanations; she presents content information to the students in final form.

The third example of an

activity reflecting a commitment to an interactive learning environment in Mr. Smith's lesson is the "forced debate." Students are assigned roles indicative of various positions within colonial society. Given that role, students must make a decision, and literally take a stand, about whether they are dissatisfied enough with the actions of the Crown, from the Navigation Acts through the implementation of the Intolerable Acts, to actively pursue independence. Mr. Smith knows that one way to help ensure that learning takes place is to ask students to use their knowledge to make decisions. Activities that encourage students to synthesize material and then take a stance provide opportunities for students to be actively engaged in the lesson. As the students *talk* about their reasons for their position, *listen* to the other side, and shape rebuttal, they are, collaboratively, constructing knowledge about the time period in a way that gives them ownership of that knowledge.

There is no such opportunity for synthesis and evaluation in Ms. Jones's class.

The *fourth* opportunity for students to actively construct knowledge within Mr. Smith's lesson occurs when he asks students to: (1) take three minutes to organize, in writing, their perceptions of the important points made during the oral discussion/debate, (2) swap what they have written with someone sitting nearby, and (3) work with that partner to revise their notes. Students are thus encouraged to use

writing as a mode of learning, as a way of capturing important ideas for future reflection, and as a way of organizing information garnered through talk that otherwise might be forgotten. Using the two language processes of *talking* and *writing* ensures cognitive processing on the part of the students because they cannot talk or write without thinking. Mr. Smith could have had students do the writing alone, without a partner, but working with a partner provides a tutorial component that reinforces learning.

There is no such opportunity to reconstruct knowledge in Ms. Jones's class.

The *fifth* way in which Mr. Smith actively involves students in the class is by asking them to determine what they have learned from the lesson. Students work together to articulate the objectives for the day, thereby indicating to themselves, and to Mr. Smith, their understanding of the purpose of the various activities in which they have been engaged. Again, students are active in the class as both *speakers* and *listeners*, speaking and listening for a stated purpose.

In Ms. Jones's class, the teacher tells the students the objectives and reiterates them at the end of the lesson, so that the students do not have to take responsibility for their learning; in Mr. Smith's class, the students, through their discussion, come to some ownership over the content of the lesson.

Finally, the *sixth* way Mr.

Smith has planned for active engagement in the lesson is by preparing students for their homework task by asking them to use the knowledge and insight gained during the class activities to craft predictions of what may "happen next" in the historical time period under discussion. Students thus have as one purpose for reading their text, to "check their predictions." Additionally, they know that they should be able to write, in their own words, a description of the first actual battle in the war. By asking students to summarize this event in their own language, Mr. Smith demonstrates that he understands that learning takes place when the learner uses language to shape experience in a personally meaningful way—and he has also helped to encourage *active reading* on the part of the students.

The writing that occurs in Ms. Jones's class does not involve the creating of meaning. Rather, students of Ms. Jones merely write what she tells them to write for the purpose of later reiterating what *she* views as important in language *she* has mandated. Although Ms. Jones does ask students to read for homework, they have no purpose for that reading and they will not be writing as they read. Some may read to memorize every detail; others will read and recall very little; some will focus on aspects of the article not directly pertinent to the purpose Ms. Jones had when she selected the homework reading; some may not read at all.

SUMMARY

In Chapter 2, you will learn more about the theory and research that supports the value of interactive instructional strategies such as those used by Mr. Smith. Chapter 2 will also help you better understand the importance of developing language-processing skills if you hope to foster students' engagement in learning. Now that you have analyzed strategies used within the context of specific lessons, try the activities listed under "Practice."

PRACTICE

1. Decide whether each of the following activities is more likely to be found in an interactive classroom or in a more passive classroom. Explain your reason by citing the nature of the language skills—listening, speaking, reading, writing—involved. Refer to Figure 1.2 in making your decision.

   • Students write questions for, and participate in, a History Bowl in order to review for the unit test.

   • The English teacher lectures on the characteristics of Romantic poetry.

   • The home economics teacher demonstrates the proper procedure for threading the sewing machine, as the students record the steps in their notebooks.

   • Students in mathematics class separate in groups of three to write the process they use to solve quadratic equations.

   • Students in science class view a film on "The Pea and Heredity."

   • Students complete rating sheets as they listen to oral reports on major composers of classical sonatas (e.g., Haydn, Mozart, Schubert, Beethoven) given by their peers in music class.

   • Students in industrial arts class use the glossary they have written as a class to verify definitions of specific tools (e.g., wood chisel, vise).

   • Students in health class read an article on stress in order to determine positive and negative stressors.

   • Students in science class label a diagram of DNA transfer as they listen to their teacher lecture on the subject.

   • Students in French I class discuss with their teacher how they might use the language other than by traveling to a French-speaking country.

   • Students in social studies class role-play Democrats and Republicans who are discussing the contra-aid scandal.

   • Students on a field trip to an art museum pause in the gallery and write for three minutes, expressing how the Impressionistic paintings of Monet make them feel.

2. The two lesson descriptions presented in this chapter are at extreme ends of the teaching continuum.

ACTIVE STUDENTS   PASSIVE STUDENTS

← X ————————————————————— X →

(Mr. Smith's lesson)   (Ms. Jones's lesson)

Mr. Smith provides multiple opportunities for students to process information and construct their own knowledge through their listening, speaking, reading, and writing skills by using writing to connect experience to content, active silent reading, reflective writing, review writing, entire class discussion and debate, and small group discussion. Ms. Jones uses some questions for the purpose of having students recall specific information in a specific sequence, and she asks students to write—but they write what she tells them to write as she talks and makes comparisons and organizes the material.

If Ms. Jones had included at least an entire class discussion during her creation of the chart, her lesson would have moved slightly toward the interactive end of the continuum.

ACTIVE STUDENTS   PASSIVE STUDENTS

←————————————————————— X ——→

(Ms. Jones's lesson
with discussion)

Select two of your university classes or two of the classes you teach. For the next week, keep a list of the activities used in each class. Refer to the active-passive charts and to the definitions of interactive classroom environments and passive classroom environments, and then decide where that class is on the teaching continuum. Share your data with another student in the class you analyzed to see if you both agree on the class's position on the continuum.

CLASSROOM CARRY-OVER

Here's how I plan to use what I just learned about active learning.

_____

_____

_____

_____

_____

_____

_____

_____

_____

_____

_____

_____

_____

_____

_____

_____

_____

_____

_____

_____

_____

_____

_____

_____

_____

_____

_____

_____

_____

_____

_____

CHAPTER₂

The Value of Interactive Instruction

What reasons do you have for promoting active learning in your classroom?

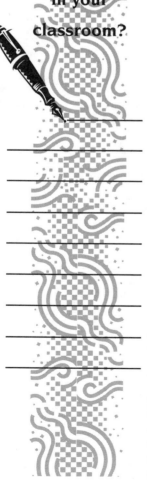

READINESS

Assume you are Mr. Smith and have been observed by your principal teaching the interactive lesson described in Chapter 1. During the debriefing of the lesson, the principal begins the discussion with this statement and question:

"Mr. Smith, you obviously made a conscious decision to teach an interactive lesson. Why? What value do you see in using this type of approach?"

Make a list of reasons you would give your principal.

Purpose for Reading

Compare your reasons for teaching an interactive lesson to those listed in Reading Material.

READING MATERIAL

Following are values that many educators place on interactive instruction.

Value #1: Facilitates the Acquisition of Content Knowledge

A primary goal for secondary teachers is to teach knowledge associated with their particular discipline. Interactive instruc-

tion facilitates the acquisition of this content information because active cognitive engagement is inherent in such instruction.

Cognitive psychology informs us that attention is a prerequisite first stage of the learning process. When students are actively engaged, their attention is maximized, and therefore, learning has a greater likelihood of occurring. In fact, the more cognitive engagement required of the learner, the greater the chances that learning will result.

Active cognitive engagement involves students in accessing what they already know about the topic to be studied. In order to process and learn new content knowledge, the learner must be able to connect the new learning with information that is already stored in memory. Otherwise, the new knowledge is nonsense, and learning and future retrieval cannot occur. This theory of learning is called *schemata theory*. Schemata represents all a person knows as stored in interconnected networks in the memory, or *cognitive structure*. Interactive instruction forces the learner to search through,

activate, retrieve, and use prior knowledge from cognitive structure. When cognitive structure is modified or elaborated upon with the help of new knowledge, learning has taken place. Through this active learning, students construct their own knowledge—content knowledge that is meaningful to them.

Because students are constructing content knowledge during their initial exposure to the content, that is, in the classroom, "studying" then becomes "review," "reinforcement," or "extension" of initial learning. When students are passive in a learning environment, they often leave the class period believing they understand the content information presented by the teacher, only to discover as they prepare for a test or application activity that, indeed, they had not learned the information. This is due to the fact that when students are passive, there is no way to ensure that they are actively engaged in tapping their backgrounds and modifying their cognitive structures. In passive learning environments, teachers deliver the results of *their* modifications of *their* cognitive structures. When this occurs, students are left to process the information on their own if they are, indeed, to learn the content information.

The acquisition of content knowledge is also facilitated by interactive instruction because this teaching approach allows for various student learning and personality styles. Interactive classrooms are places where students with visual, auditory, or kinesthetic perceptual preferences have ample opportunities to become involved meaningfully in the lessons. There are also opportunities for students with various sociological stimuli preferences to think and work alone as well as with a partner, a small group of peers, and with the entire class. Because strategies are varied in an interactive environment, at some point in the lesson, all students are provided with the learning circumstances that best support their chances of efficiently and effectively processing and constructing content knowledge.

Another way that interactive instruction facilitates the acquisition of content knowledge is through the direct and immediate feedback on their responses that students receive from the teacher and peers. Because so much oral and written communication takes place in this type of instruction, students profit from receiving immediate feedback about whether they are "on track." If the teacher discovers through student responses that students are not learning or are learning incorrect information, the teacher can imme-diately adapt the instruction, for example, through a new activity or additional questioning, in order to shape and facilitate the learning of appropriate content information. Thus, an inefficient situation in which students process incorrect content knowledge is avoided. When such a situation is discovered later by the teacher, students must unlearn and relearn the information correctly.

Finally, interactive instruction also facilitates the learning of content knowledge because such classrooms are "busy" places—places where students spend maximum classroom time "on task." Interactive lessons often include several different activities during one class period. The lessons move smoothly from activity to activity, thereby not allowing time for students to disengage their attention from the learning taking place. Such "time on task," that is, the time students are directly engaged in meaningful academic tasks and doing so with success, is directly related to success in student achievement.

Value #2: Sharpens Students' Thinking Skills

Interactive classrooms provide continuous opportunities for students to think, that is to make meaning of their world. They use critical and creative thinking skills and strategies in order to form concepts and principles, to solve problems, to make decisions, to use suspended judgment and evaluation, and to create something new.

To practice thinking, students need a setting where listening, speaking, reading, and writing are encouraged, where numerous questions are asked, where creative and critical thinking are valued, and where students have opportunities to solve relevant problems for themselves.

In this age of information explosion, we must give students reasoning strategies that will enable them to think systematically and independently in school as well as later in life as adults and citizens. Unfortunately, a majority of secondary classrooms are not places where student independent thinking is fostered. Too often it is only the teachers who think, then present their thinking in final form to the students through passive instruction. Such instruction does nothing to free students from reliance on others for decisions. Additionally, denying students opportunities to engage in independent reasoning denies them the joy of discovery and problem solving and the development of confidence in their ability to think for themselves.

Thinking is a learned skill and a highly active process. Through interactive instruction, students are afforded maximum opportunities to practice thinking.

Value #3: Develops Students' Language-Processing Skills

Students improve their ability to use the language-processing skills of listening, speaking, reading, and writing through practice. In an interactive setting, students receive frequent practice in these four, all-important learning and life skills.

The receptive language processes of listening and reading open doors for students to be exposed to new information and opinions. Listening relies on auditory messages; reading relies on visual images. Both listening and reading require the learner to comprehend, thus for both processes the learner must have a purpose for listening/reading and must construct meaning.

The productive language processes of speaking and writing provide students opportunities to express and test their information and opinions. Like listening and reading, speaking and writing are aural and visual counterparts. Both require the learner to have a purpose for generating the message and a responsibility to send a coherent message.

In an interactive classroom, these four language processes are often used in complementary ways. For example, students may *read* and *write* their reaction to the reading, then share (*speak*) their written reaction with a peer who must *listen*, then respond orally (speak). Or, students may *listen* to a student presentation or discussion (*speak*), then *write* a summary of the key points noted.

One of the important features of interactive instruction is the way the teacher sets up speaking situations in the lessons. In a passive classroom, the teacher out-talks the students, and if the students engage in talk, it is usually directed to the teacher in response to his/her questions. Even in an entire class discussion, the teacher does most of the talking. Speaking in an interactive classroom engages students in conversation with peers as well as with the teacher. Called "collaborative learning," this activity involves small groups of students talking out a problem. Of course, this collaborative learning requires listening, and often the talking is done in conjunction with reading and/or writing to complete the activity. When teachers create instructional settings in which students "talk to learn," but in which they also work together to accomplish a particular goal for which they take joint responsibility and toward which they each contribute in individually accountable ways, "cooperative learning" occurs.

Frequent and purposeful talking is an essential attribute of interactive instruction. Talking facilitates problem solving; talking externalizes thought; talking allows students to shape and evaluate their own thoughts as they hear them for the first time with their spoken voice and to have their ideas validated or challenged by their peers. Through discussion, students in the group use their own linguistic networks (language that makes sense to them) to grapple with a problem and to reshape ideas. The result is learning, adaptation of their cognitive structures, because the language they used to solve the problem came from their linguistic networks, not from that of the teacher, which may not match those of the students.

Value #4: Enhances Students' Social Skills and Self-Esteem

By now it should be obvious that interactive classrooms are "live" places. In these classrooms, students have frequent opportunities to collaborate or construct knowledge through verbal interaction, while they work in cooperative arrangements—small groups of students who work together to accomplish a goal. Such collaborative learning fosters positive peer working relationships and self-esteem as well as increases motivation and promotes achievement, language processing, and critical thinking skills.

Interactive classrooms emphasize democratic social relationships where students must practice self-control in order to contribute to the successful completion of the activity and the learning of the content knowledge. In interactive classrooms, students are partners in the learning process; in passive classrooms, the teacher is the primary source of the knowledge. When students shoulder increased responsibility for the thinking that takes place during the lesson, they feel positive about their capabilities as learners. Armed with this "can do" attitude, students tend to demonstrate maturity and self-reliance in the interactive classroom. As a result of this positive climate, interactive classrooms are exciting environments in which to work.

SUMMARY

In this chapter, you have learned about the theoretical and research support for the concept of an interactive classroom. You should now recognize that students who participate actively in their learning through engaging in listening, speaking, reading, and writing activities reap many benefits: 1) they acquire important content knowledge; 2) they sharpen thinking skills; 3) they practice language-processing skills; and 4) they enhance social skills and self-esteem.

RESOURCES

The following readings provide a more in-depth discussion of the theory and research that undergirds the value of interactive instruction.

Facilitating the Acquisition of Content Knowledge

- Barnes, D., Britton, J., and Torbe, M. *Language, Learner, and the School*. Portsmouth, N.H.: Boyton Cook, 1990.
- Berliner, D. "Tempus Educare." In *Research on Teaching: Concepts, Findings and Implications*, P. Peterson and H. Walberg, eds. Berkeley, Calif.: McCutchan, 1979.
- Dunn, R., Beadry, J., and Klavas, A. "Survey of Research on Learning Styles." *Educational Leadership* 46 (1989): 50–53.
- Fischer, C., Filby, N., Marliave, R., Cahen, L., Dishaw, M., Moore, J., and Berliner, D. "Teaching Behaviors, Academic Learning Time, and Student Achievement." Final report of *Phase III-B, Beginning Teacher Evaluation Study*. San Francisco: Far West Laboratory for Educational Research and Development, 1978.
- Kagan, J. "Learning, Attention, and the Issue of Discovery." In *Learning by Discovery: A Critical Appraisal*, edited by L.S. Shulman and E.R. Keislar. Chicago: Rand McNally, 1966.
- Resnick, L.B. *Education and Learning to Think*. Washington, D.C.: National Academy Press, 1987.
- Smith, F. *Comprehension and Learning: A Conceptual Framework for Teachers*. New York: Holt, Rinehart, and Winston, 1975.
- Smith, F. *To Think*. New York: Teachers College Press, 1990.
- Stallings, J. "Allocated Academic Learning Time Revisited, or Beyond Time on Task." *Educational Researcher* 9 (1980): 11–16.

Developing Students' Thinking Skills

- Beyer, B.K. *Practical Strategies for the Teaching of Thinking*. Boston: Allyn and Bacon, 1987.
- Costa, A.L. *Developing Minds: A Resource Book for Teaching Thinking*. Alexandria, Va.: Association for Supervision and Curriculum Development, 1985.
- Dewey, J. *How We Think*. Boston: D.C. Heath, 1910.
- Joyce, B., and Weil, M. *Models of Teaching*. Englewood Cliffs, N.J.: Prentice-Hall, 1980.
- Marzano, R.J., Brandt, R.S., Hughes, C.S., Jones, B.F., Presseisen, B.Z., Rankin, S.C., and Suhor, C. *Dimensions of Thinking: A Framework for Curriculum and Instruction*. Alexandria, Va.: Association for Supervision and Curriculum Development, 1988.
- McTighe, J. "The Need to Improve Student Thinking: A Rationale Statement." Baltimore: Maryland State Department of Education, n.d. (photocopy).
- Neilsen, A.R. "Critical Thinking and Reading: Empowering Learners to Think and Act." In *Teaching Critical Thinking*, no. 2. Bloomington, Ind.: ERIC Clearinghouse on Reading and Communication Skills, and Urbana, Ill.: National Council of Teachers of English, 1989.
- Neubert, G.A., and Binko, J.B. *Encouraging Inductive Reasoning in the Secondary School*. Washington, D.C.: National Education Association, 1992.
- Smith, Frank. "The Politics of Ignorance." In *Essays into Literacy*, edited by F. Smith. Portsmouth, N.H.: Heinemann, 1983.
- __. *Insult to Intelligence*. Portsmouth, N.H.: Heinemann, 1986.

Developing Students' Language Processing Skills

- Barnes, D. *From Communication to Curriculum*. New York: Penguin Books, 1984.

- Berthoff, A.E., ed. *Reclaiming the Imagination: Philosophical Perspectives on Writers and Teachers of Writing*. Upper Montclair, N.J.: Boynton Cook, 1984.

- Britton, J. *Language and Learning*. Harmondsworth, England: Pelican Books, 1970.

- Bruffee, K.A. "Collaborative Learning and the 'Conversations of Mankind.'" *College English* 46 (1984): 635–52.

- Gagne, R.M., and Smith, E.C., Jr. "A Study of the Effects of Verbalization on Problem Solving." *Journal of Experimental Psychology* 63 (1962): 12–18.

- Lundsteen, S.W. "Learning to Listen and Learning to Read." In *Perspectives on Talk and Learning*, edited by S. Hynds and D.L. Rubin. Urbana, Ill.: National Council of Teachers of English, 1990.

- Vygotsky, L.S. *Mind in Society: The Development of Higher Psychological Processes*. Cambridge, Mass.: Harvard University Press, 1978.

Enhancing Students' Social Skills and Self-Esteem

- Golub, J. (chair) and the Committee on Classroom Practices. *Focus on Collaborative Learning*. Urbana, Ill.: National Council of Teachers of English, 1988.

- Johnson, D.W., Johnson, R.T., Holubec, E.J., and Roy, P. *Circles of Learning: Cooperation in the Classroom*. Alexandria, Va.: Association for Supervision and Curriculum Development, 1984.

- Purkey, W.W. *Self-Concept and School Achievement*. Englewood Cliffs, N.J.: Prentice-Hall, 1970.

- Slavin, R.E. *Cooperative Learning*. New York: Longman, 1983.

- __. *Educational Psychology: Theory into Practice*. Englewood Cliffs, N.J.: Prentice-Hall, 1986.

PRACTICE

1. Go back to Mr. Smith's lesson and determine:

   • how he helps students at the beginning of this learning experience to tap their backgrounds of experience so the new content knowledge will be meaningful to them

   • what activities he uses to ensure that students with various learning and personality styles are accommodated

   • where in the lesson students receive feedback on their responses from him and also from peers

   • how many different activities the students engage in during this one lesson

   • where he provides opportunities for the students to think independently of him

   • where students listen, talk to him, talk to their peers, read, and write

   • where the students have opportunities to work collaboratively in small groups.

2. Go to Chapter 5 and read the Directed Reading Activity Plans on pp. 83-86. How would you answer the preceding seven questions for this lesson?

CLASSROOM CARRY-OVER

Here's how I plan to use what I just learned about interactive learning.

_____
_____
_____
_____
_____
_____
_____
_____
_____
_____
_____
_____
_____
_____
_____
_____
_____
_____
_____
_____
_____
_____
_____
_____
_____
_____
_____
_____
_____
_____
_____
_____

Listening in the Interactive Classroom

How do you encourage students to be effective listeners?

READINESS

Complete Figure 3.1, (next page) indicating what the teacher and students do when the following techniques are used in the classroom: lecturing, demonstrating, showing films or videos or using other audiovisual aids, taking field trips, giving oral reports, and role-playing. Do you see any patterns here? What do these strategies all require of students? What is the primary language-processing skill they must use in order for learning to occur?

Purpose for Reading

What is involved in the listening process, and what does research tell us about reasons students do not always develop effective listening skills? What do we know about why it is important to enhance students' abilities as listeners? How can teachers prepare students to listen so that they can become more active participants in the lesson? How can teachers enhance students' effectiveness as listeners during a class session in which students are primarily listening to learn? Answers to these questions are found in the Reading Material section of this chapter.

READING MATERIAL

This section takes a comprehensive look at the listening process and its relationship to learning.

The Listening Process And the Value of Listening to Learn

The listening process involves attending to auditory stimuli (hearing) and then attempting to understand and interpret the meaning of these stimuli. To be done well, listening also requires that the listener block out stimuli that bear no relationship to the message being delivered (for instance, the sound of the television in the background during a telephone conversation), differentiate between the intellectual and emotional content of the message, and whenever possible, add to the auditory message information acquired through interpretation of the speaker's body language.

Many teachers know that students become oblivious to the stream of talk to which, in more traditional classrooms, they are subjected each day. Adler and Towne (1987) report on research conducted by Paul Cameron. Cameron examined what 85 college students were actually thinking about during his lecture course in psychology. When a gun was fired at random, often in the middle of a sentence, students encoded their thoughts at that moment. At any given moment, 20 percent of the students were pursuing erotic thoughts; 20 percent were reminiscing about something; only 12 percent were actively listening to the lecture; the rest were worrying about something or daydreaming. What this study indicates is that without real listening, the stream of talk that surrounds students in many classrooms as teachers lecture, use demonstrations, or show films, does little to contribute to their knowledge base, and so does little to further their education. As Verderber and Verderber (1986) note, listening provides people with the data they need in order to respond to each other, although they find that people listen with only 20 to 50 percent efficiency. On a positive note, listening is a skill that can be learned, and, when students are helped to focus their listening, they become more productive participants in the interactive classroom (Devine 1978).

Inhibitors to Good Listening
Recall Ms. Jones' lesson in Chapter 1. Here are some additional pieces of information about the students in Ms. Jones' class and about their en-

Strategy	Teacher Actions	Student Actions
Lecture	_____	_____
	_____	_____
Demonstration	_____	_____
	_____	_____
Movies/Videos/ Other Audiovisuals	_____	_____
	_____	_____
Field Trips	_____	_____
	_____	_____
Oral Reports	_____	_____
	_____	_____
Role Play	_____	_____
	_____	_____

Figure 3.1
Classroom Techniques and
Related Actions.
How would you complete
this chart?

vironment. As you read through this list, try to determine some of the factors that may prevent any given student from attending as Ms. Jones delivers her lesson, a lesson that is heavily laced with teacher talk.

1. This lesson is taking place during the last period of the day.

2. During the three periods prior to this one, Ms. Jones's students: (a) participated in physical fitness testing in their physical education class, (b) took a math quiz, and (c) completed a lab in earth science.

3. Waseem, who arrived in the United States from Syria six months ago, is part of this class. He was only recently mainstreamed into it from an "English as a Second Language" class.

4. Karen is also part of this class. She has considerable hearing loss in both ears, and she is accompanied by her interpreter.

5. The temperature is 95 degrees. The school has no air conditioning, so Ms. Jones has opened the windows, thus allowing the noise of Farmer Brown's tractor to fill the air as he plows the field next to the school site, along with the noise of students participating in an outdoor gym class.

6. Also, recognize that Ms. Jones is teaching U.S. history to middle school students who have heard about the founding of this country in almost all of their grade-school classes.

What are some of the factors you noted that may interfere with students' abilities to process information through listening as they participate in Ms. Jones' class? Why is it so difficult to listen actively, and why should teachers encourage students to "listen to learn"? Adler and Towne (1987) outline nine different causes of poor listening, many of which are inherent in the scenario of Ms. Jones' classroom.

1. First of all, the amount of speech we hear every day is enormous. We spend at least five hours a day listening to people talk. Thus, it is difficult to listen carefully to everything that is said because of message overload.

2. Often, it is difficult to attend to a speaker because fatigue or personal problems and worries cause us to be preoccupied.

3. Similarly, the sounds of the environment may cause us to be preoccupied; external noise surrounding a speaker's words, such as music in the background, other conversations, traffic noises, or even the sound of a pencil scratching across a paper, can interfere with the ability to attend to the speaker.

4. It is hard to attend to a speaker for physiological reasons, too. Bradley (1991) notes that while we are capable of listening to up to 600 words per minute, speakers only produce between 100 and 140 words per minute. Thus, the listener has a great deal of storage space in his or her mind to spare, which he or she is likely to fill with thoughts not directly related to what the speaker is saying.

5. We also know that listening well requires a great deal of hard work. Nichols (1977) shows that when a listener is active, truly listening, the heart rate quickens, body temperature rises, and respiration increases—all changes we usually associate with physical labor!

6. Also, we make faulty assumptions about either the content of the speaker's message or about our own abilities to comprehend it that interfere with our abilities to make sense of that message. Abrell

(1984) and Nelson and Heeney (1984) find that cultural differences influence misunderstandings as do "internal noise levels." The student who attempts to hear a teacher explain a mathematical procedure while thinking, "I'm no good at math; I'll never get this!" probably never will. Likewise, the student who hears the college professor lecturing on the Civil War while thinking, "I've heard this stuff since I was seven!" probably will not recognize that additional material is being presented—or that the material is being analyzed in a more complex, sophisticated way.

7. Adler and Towne (1987) also note that we readily perceive the advantages of being the speaker. When speaking, we can persuade or make our point of view known; we can gain others' respect for our intellect or wit by telling jokes or explaining a procedure; we can release our frustrations and talk through a problem to a solution. Students often, then, perceive that listening has a lack of apparent advantages. However, students need to learn that being a good listener is one significant trait associated with being perceived as a good friend and that being willing to listen is perceived as a powerful strategy in getting others to listen to their ideas. Listening is a way to gain the respect and confidence of superiors, peers, and subordinates (Hinds and Pankake 1987).

8. Obviously, a student with hearing problems will not be served well by teaching strategies that demand listening as the primary mode of learning.

9. Finally, lack of training in listening also contributes to students' failure to learn through listening. Students need direct instruction focused on helping them learn to attend, identify key information, and organize information perceived to be important. (Adler and Towne 1987).

Strategies Used to Avoid Real Listening
Imagine you are an observer in Mr. Smith's classroom as he teaches the lesson described in Chapter 1. For the most part, his students do seem to be actively engaged in the learning process, but you notice the following student behaviors during the lesson.

1. Whenever Mr. Smith asks a question, David drops his eyes to his paper and moves his hand across it rapidly.

2. While Mr. Smith, or another student, is talking, Kim makes direct eye contact with the speaker, nods, and smiles—but, you notice at one point that her "yes" head gesture does not seem an appropriate response to the comment just made.

3. Jim is staring out the window, following Farmer Brown's tractor as it goes up and down the field next to the school, plowing under the stubble of last year's crop.

Ask yourself how these students are avoiding real listening. Brainstorm about reasons you, or other listeners you know, may fail to listen effectively. There are a number of such strategies used by listeners to avoid "really listening."

1. Some seem to listen, but are really playing the "looking busy" game. They nod, smile, jot down notes at certain intervals during the lecture or discussion, but in actuality, something else in their minds is occupying the majority of their attention. Students who employ this strategy go home in the evenings to find they have a page full of notes that are fragmentary and incomprehensible.

2. Some students are selective in their listening; they tune into a presentation when something of interest is mentioned, and they tune out everything else. For this type of student, the use of examples drawn from real life that help them relate to the material in a personal way is an important tool in getting them to remain open to the presentation of material.

3. Other students listen attentively, but only to gather material to use in attacking the speaker later. This type of listener is likely to misinterpret the speaker or to record only that information he or she can use in generating a counterargument. Such listeners fail to listen to the logic of the speaker's presentation. Thus, these students need to hear oral discussions that acknowledge opposing points of view and that model how a particular stance has been developed.

4. Many more students are likely to be "passive listeners," listeners who try to take in a teacher's comments without

the benefit of verbal manipulation of those comments (e.g., without using the information later in discussion). Thus, misunderstandings develop. The teacher tells the students, "Poe was the father of detective fiction," and the students write down, "Poe's father wrote detective stories." Or, the teacher becomes temporarily tongue-tied and makes an inaccurate statement, such as "Columbus sailed the ocean blue in 1592," which the students write down as fact because they are not thinking about the implications of the statement. Or, the teacher makes a statement, open to a variety of interpretations, such as "It is difficult to begin a complete sentence with the word *because*," and a student internalizes the message as, "I can't ever use *because* at the beginning of a sentence."

In none of these examples are students learning effectively. To become better learners, these students need to become better listeners. They need to become better able to take in information, to process it, to make sense of it, to be able to retrieve it, and then to use it in a variety of circumstances. They need to have their poor listening habits pointed out to them; they need supervised practice in developing good listening habits; and they need teachers who demand that they maintain mental engagement in the learning process as they listen actively to classroom discourse. They also need teachers who are themselves models for how to listen actively. In

short, teachers and students need to recognize that active listening is often the first step in constructing knowledge. Teachers and students need to understand that without listening, students' visual images often do not make sense to them, and that without explanation, textual material may often be misinterpreted. Without listening to others, students are limited to their own sense of reality when they seek to define and attack a problem.

Types of Listening

Make a list of the times during your typical day when you devote your energy primarily to listening. After making this list, write a sentence or two in which you generalize about the different purposes you have for listening to different types of material. Do your purposes match those that follow?

Students need to know that there are different ways of listening just as there are different ways of reading, each of which is appropriate in different settings.

1. Sometimes, we listen just for appreciation or enjoyment. This is the type of listening that occurs when, after a hard or frustrating day, we listen to a favorite piece of music and allow ourselves to feel it, to relax and flow with the music. Or, it is the type of listening we do when we listen to a joke.

2. Sometimes, we listen to take in information. This type of listening is required when we need instructions about

how to do a particular task, or when we need directions in order to arrive at a specific destination. It is also the type of listening for details students must often do in order to create a basis of information from which they later must argue, make comparisons, or form judgments.

3. Listening for details frequently, then, leads to listening for understanding. This is the type of listening students must engage in when they are presented with many points of view, many theories, or many examples, and then asked to formulate their own opinion or to generate their own hypotheses.

Note that the first purpose for listening listed here requires little of the student except attention and immediate response; the other two require a different type of attention, frequently involving the taking of notes or the asking of questions. Students need to recognize the differences.

Getting Ready to Listen

There are several major teaching strategies that depend on students' ability to listen in order to learn: lecture/lecture-demonstration, field trips, role play and simulations, large group discussion, small group discussion, student presentations, and the use of audiovisual materials. No matter which of these strategies the teacher selects, he or she must prepare the students to attend to the verbal information that will comprise the majority of the lesson content. If such preparation is not completed, students are likely to fall into the ineffective listening patterns previously outlined. The following techniques may be used by teachers who desire to activate and then focus their students' attention prior to engaging them in a listening task: (1) tapping prior experience and tapping prior knowledge and (2) purpose setting, including purpose setting for listening to the teacher, listening to other students making presentations, listening to a role play, or watching and listening to audiovisual material through giving instructions, asking questions, or making a controversial statement.

Tapping Prior Experience

Imagine an eighth grade math teacher who begins her class by asking that all the female students move to the left side of the room and that all the males move to the right. Then she asks all students who are involved in any type of sports activity (or music activity, part-time work, etc.) to move to the back of the room. It is likely that there will be both male and female students moving at this point. The students return to their seats, and the teacher proceeds to use this experience as the basis for developing the lesson content for the day: the intersection and unions of sets.

This same teacher could have begun class by discussing the sorting of laundry, asking what types of items students would put into each of three loads of wash and then how they would regroup if they discovered they had only enough money (or detergent) to do

two loads of laundry. Or, she could have asked students to discuss how they choose pizza to purchase for a party when they know some of their friends like pepperoni on pizza, some like mushrooms, some like plain cheese, and so forth. Whatever approach this teacher takes, the result is the same: students will be prepared to listen to an expository explanation of set theory because they can relate the abstractions of the lesson to their own experience.

Some teachers provide classroom experiences upon which they can build when they deliver new material. For instance, prior to initiating a discussion of the Robert Frost poem, "Mending Wall," which contains the line, "Good fences make good neighbors," a student teacher engaged students' attention through an unusual activity. Typically, in this teacher's classroom after lunch, students entered the classroom, deposited their books at their desks and then returned to the hall to use the restroom or to socialize. On this day, the student teacher moved individual student's belongings from one desk to another, and she also pushed the desks, usually in rows, together so that they touched. Upon reentering the room, students quickly spotted what they perceived as disarray and put the room back into its usual state. Class began, and the student teacher asked students what they had noticed about the classroom, and why they had put it back into its traditional format. She then

used their answers as an anchor for the discussion of the Frost poem that followed, always tying the students' response to and analysis of the poem back to their experience at the beginning of the class session.

The math teacher and English teacher described here have tapped prior experience by discussing with students real-life situations in which they may have had to use concepts drawn from set theory and by relating a classroom experience to the message of a literary piece. In Chapter 1, Mr. Smith did something similar when he had students write about feeling independent/dependent.

It is also possible to tap students' experience by asking them to brainstorm what they already know about a topic. For instance, a geography teacher could lead the class in brainstorming on "Brazil," "volcanoes," or "longitude and latitude." As the students listen to the teacher's presentation, their job is to verify their existing knowledge base and to add to it.

Some teachers extend the technique of tapping prior knowledge by then asking students, either individually or as a group, to generate questions they have about a topic. For instance, students might know that Brazil is in South America, and they might note that the country is frequently in the news because of concern over the loss of its rain forests. As a result, they may ask, "What is a rain forest? Why is it so important to the earth's ecology?" Now, when they attend to the content of the lesson, they not only attempt to verify what they think they "know," but they attempt to answer their own questions, questions that have been developed out of their own prior experiences.

Purpose Setting

Strategies designed to tap prior experience are related to that of purpose setting, and both approaches are applications of the concept of "advanced organizer" as defined by Ausabel (1980) and tested for effectiveness with students of all ability levels, including those with special needs (Gleason 1988, Reetz and Hoover 1989). When the teacher wants the students to listen, either to teacher talk, student talk, or the auditory messages of a film or video, the teacher can help the students attend to key points by giving instructions that provide them with a reason or focus for their listening. You will read in Chapter 5 about the concept of "purpose setting" as it applies to guiding students' reading of a text—a strategy employed within this text. Here are several examples of such instruction.

1. "As you watch the film, listen for the five reasons provided for the cause of the Civil War."

2. "Listen to this dialogue of two native Spanish speakers, one from Mexico and one from Spain, and jot down at least two ways in which their pronunciation is different."

3. "I will outline two methods for solving systems of equations and will detail the types of situations in which each should be used. Write down the steps in both methods and note when each is most appropriately applied."

Also, when students are to listen to each other as they deliver oral reports and serve as the "experts" during class, the teacher can provide a similar type of guidance. For instance, when students are giving oral reports about American novels written between the two world wars they have read for their independent reading project, the teacher might say, "As each student talks about his or her book, jot down the major theme mentioned. We will see if we can draw any conclusions about the themes important to American novelists of this period." Or, when an art class is delivering presentations about major artists of the Cubist movement, the teacher might tell those listening, "As each student presents the results of his or her research, jot down the major contributions of each artist, titles of major works, and ways in which each artist adapted or extended or revised the principles of Cubism to suit his or her own purposes."

The same type of guidance may be given by providing a question or questions students should seek to answer. These questions may be presented orally or in worksheet fashion. As students watch the film version of *To Kill a Mockingbird* after having read the Harper Lee novel in their English class, they might have a series of questions to answer designed, overall, to help them compare and contrast the two art forms. The guide sheet might include such questions as, "How does the opening of the film set the mood and establish the setting for the story? How does the text do so? What are the key events shown in the film? Are there any events from the novel that have been deleted or shortened? Why do you think the screenplay differed from the novel in terms of content? What was the effect, when reading the novel, of having the missing scenes available to you? How is the characterization of Atticus Finch achieved through the acting of Gregory Peck? How is this characterization similar to and/or different from the images you created of Atticus while you read?" And, "Overall, if you had to choose to purchase for your own home either the film or the novel of *To Kill a Mockingbird*, which would it be and why? Exclude price as a determining factor."

Similarly, the teacher might provide a purpose for listening by beginning an oral presentation with a controversial or provocative statement. A math teacher who announces at the beginning of a class, "The invention of the zero was one of the most significant human achievements of all time," or the history teacher who says emphatically, "The South should have won the Civil War" will grab the attention of students who will listen in a focused way, attempting to discover the reasons for the speaker's opinions.

The examples given here are examples of the adaptation of the concepts of "skimming" and "scanning," usually applied to the act of reading, to the development of "purpose for listening" frameworks (Joiner, Adkins, and Eykyn 1989). Other listening activities that would help students practice *scanning auditory material*, that is, listening for specific elements of information, might include

- matching exercises,
- a checklist on which students would check those ideas or terms that they encounter, or
- fill-in-the blank guides.

Other activities that would involve students in *general scanning*, that is, listening for the overall meaning or gist of discourse, might include telling students to:

- listen to determine the general purpose of the talk (Is the speaker seeking to explain, persuade, entertain?)
- listen to determine which of several pictures best illustrates the main ideas of the oral text
- select the best title for the oral text
- define key terms from the context clues provided by the speaker.

Similarly, students who are not actors in a role play should be provided with a purpose for viewing and listening. For example, students might be directed to do the following.

- Write down times during the role play when they felt the actors were not faithful to the information they were provided about an historical incident.
- Note times when they felt the plot of the scenario could have been developed in a different direction.
- List examples of times when the actors either listened attentively to each other or times when the actors' verbal communication contrasted with their body language.

Providing a purpose for listening for the audience about to view the role play helps maintain students' interest and attention, so that everyone in the class, not merely those actually engaged in the role play, learn from the experience. The same reasoning holds for providing a purpose for listening when the teacher is using filmstrips accompanied by a recorded or live reading of explanatory text, slide/tape presentations, films, or videos. At times, the novelty of these materials is enough to stimulate initial interest. However, because they are frequently overused, or used in ineffective ways without much thought as to the relationship between the experiences provided and the objectives of the lesson, students often view the turning out of the lights as a signal for sleeping, writing notes, or doing other homework.

Thus, when teachers use audiovisual materials, they should follow three major guidelines.

1. Provide students with a reason for viewing and listening.

2. Hold students accountable for the content in some way.

3. Teach students how to be discriminating listeners and viewers by

- asking them, for instance, to note how the use of background music contributes to the overall mood of the film, or how it serves to underscore important points in a video,
- providing outlines for students to complete while they listen and watch,
- asking students to attempt to define significant vocabulary from the context provided, both verbal and visual, in a filmstrip or movie,
- indicating how the material provided through the use of the audiovisual aids relates to the objectives for the lesson and to the goals for the unit, and
- accompanying the use of a filmstrip, film, video, audiotape or other recording with teacher talk that can help students attend more effectively to those aspects of the movie or filmstrip that relate to the class objectives.

Enhancing the Processing Of Information While Students Are Engaged in Listening

Recall the descriptions of students in Ms. Jones' and Mr. Smith's classrooms provided at the beginning of this chapter. If you were one of these teachers and realized, in the middle of an activity during which students were supposed to be listening in order to learn, that their attention was wandering, what could you do? How can a teacher help students process information more effectively while they are listening, or refocus their attention during a listening activity? Sometimes it just is not enough to deliver "purpose for listening" instructions or to provide a guide for students to complete while listening. Sometimes, students need help in processing the auditory information they are receiving so that they do not merely hear it, but make sense of it. The following strategies will be described, all of which can help students refocus and increase listening comprehension: (1) asking questions, (2) guiding reflection and note taking, (3) guiding attention during discussion through the use of graphic organizers, (4) using visual reinforcements, and (5) encouraging active listening.

Asking Questions
Cognitive psychologists tell us that after 20 minutes or so of listening, "cognitive overload" begins. If we ask students to listen for too long a stretch of time without providing some sort of break, they have difficulty, for the reasons outlined at the beginning of this chapter, in continuing to attend to auditory stimuli. Pausing in the middle of a lecture to ask real questions that help students synthesize the information they have already heard and that help them begin to

use that information as a basis for what they will hear next, is one simple but important technique. An art teacher might stop a filmstrip about the Impressionists to ask, "What are the major features of Impressionist work?" And, the teacher might establish a new purpose for listening for the rest of the filmstrip: "As we move into a discussion of Seurat, keep track of the ways in which he did or did not exhibit those major features of Impressionism in his work."

Also, during a lecture, discussion, film, or any type of auditory-based lesson, the teacher can ask questions designed to reconnect the world of the students' experience to the content of that lesson. For instance, after having presented material on "set theory" in the lesson described earlier in this chapter, the teacher might stop the lesson to ask the students when and how in their everyday lives they use the concepts and principles involved in the lesson. Or, having delivered a talk on the food chain, the biology teacher might ask students to predict how the food chain in their local community has been altered by a particular recent event, such as the construction of a new housing project.

Guiding Reflection
Asking questions is but one strategy designed to help students reflect on material presented verbally so that they have some guidance for processing it effectively and meaningfully. Teachers can

also ask students to *write* about material they have been hearing, perhaps in a reflective journal, through the Cornell system of note taking, through the use of paragraph frames, or through the strategy of having a class recorder.

1. Reflective Journal: A reflective journal can be used in the following ways.

- In the middle of a heated discussion, when the teacher is afraid that the class is going off the topic or is becoming so emotionally involved in the topic that the main arguments for both sides are being lost in the rhetoric, he or she can stop the student talk for a few minutes while students are guided to list the major points that have been made or to summarize what they have learned about the topic at hand.
- If the teacher, or a student, is delivering information in a lecture format, students might be asked to write down (possibly by reviewing the notes they have been taking) the three (or some more appropriate number) major ideas or to outline the steps in the process being explained as they understand them.
- During a discussion, lecture, or other auditory event, instead of asking, "Are there any questions?"—to which students typically do not respond—the teacher can

ask students to generate at least three questions they have about what has already been said or about what they may still want to know.

- Students might even be asked to create a test question based on the discussion that the teacher may use in creating a quiz or test for the class.

2. Cornell Note-Taking System: Pauk (1984) describes the Cornell System for guiding note taking, which is also designed to help students reflect upon and synthesize information they have acquired through the listening process. As the student listens, he or she takes notes in simple paragraph (or in another comfortable format) on the right-hand side of a sheet of paper, leaving a left margin of two and a half to three inches. After listening to a lecture, viewing a film, or participating in a discussion, the student skims the notes, jotting key words or phrases in the left-hand margin as a way to spark recall of the material. Finally, either in a third column on the right side of the page or in a space left underneath the notes and key words, the student summarizes the material, using the key words as a catalyst for reviewing and reiterating the content of the lesson when he or she is studying alone, perhaps at home. The framework of the student's paper thus resembles the framework illustrated in Figure 3.2.

3. Paragraph Frames: Some students need more structure than the Cornell system provides, especially when they are just learning how to take notes while listening for key information. Studies have shown that within two weeks, students typically forget at least 80 percent of what they have heard; within four weeks, barely five percent remains (Langan 1987). Thus, students need help in learning how to listen for the purpose of taking notes. Nichols (1980) describes paragraph frames as a technique for helping remedial students with writing assignments. This strategy can also be adapted to help students with listening assignments. The teacher provides a paragraph with key words and items deleted and blank space for their insertion, so that as students listen to a lecture, oral report, oral reading of a text, or the sound track of a movie or filmstrip, they plug in the terms. Initially, the paragraph frame serves as a "purpose for listening" device because students skim the frame before listening in order to get an idea of the blank spaces they will have to fill. As they listen, the frame guides their attention and keeps it focused on the listening task at hand. This strategy is especially valuable

for students who need a great deal of structure. For example, Forster and Doyle (1989) offer proof that providing an outline to students diagnosed with attention deficit disorders helps their listening skills. An example of a paragraph frame is provided in Figure 3.3.

Key Words	Discussion/Lecture/Viewing Notes	Summary

Figure 3.2
Framework Used in Cornell Note-Taking System.

The **Tropic of Cancer** crosses Mexico. Thus, most of the country lies in the **tropics** or **subtropics**. However, due to dramatic differences in **altitude** across the country, Mexico has a great variety of climate. At the **northern** part of the Central Plateau, the visitor will experience a hot, dry **desert** climate. As the visitor moves southward on the plateau, the climate becomes **temperate**. We would expect to become hotter during the move southward as we approach the **tropics**, but the high altitude of the plateau causes a **moderation** of temperature.

(**Note:** The boldface words would not appear in the copy of the paragraph frame provided to students. Students would see blank spaces on their papers, and they would listen to fill in the spaces as the teacher delivered the information.)

Figure 3.3
Paragraph Frame For the Beginning Of a Lecture on "The Climate of Mexico"

As students develop their skill as listeners, the frame provided can become less and less detailed. Some teachers provide a blank outline for students to complete as they listen. The outline contains only the Roman numerals and the letters and numbers the teacher deems appropriate. Some teachers provide even less guidance, merely identifying key words or concepts on the chalkboard or on the overhead. Students are then told that any item so noted should go into their notes (written in their own words), along with any related information they deem important. No matter how little structure is provided, the students should listen more effectively because the structure helps them determine before they listen what is important and deserves attention, and what is extraneous.

4. Class Recorder: Another variation on note taking that encourages active listening is that of class recorder. Teachers who use class recorders do so because they want individual students to have the opportunity to write for a real audience, in this case their peers, and thus to take responsibility for organizing information in a fashion that is easily accessible and comprehensible to that audience. Students either volunteer to serve as class recorder on specific dates, or the teacher makes the assignments. The class recorder is responsible for keeping track of the objectives of the class, for keeping track of major terms used in the class period and defining them, for writing down major points made in class, and for listing handouts given and assignments made during the class period. These notes are then collected (and graded by the teacher if she or he so desires) and put into a class notebook, along with samples of the handouts provided during the class session. Students in class serving as recorder know that others are depending on them for this service and thus have an incentive to do their job well.

Guiding Attention and Reflection Through the Use Of Graphic Organizers

A variation of the paragraph-frame strategy involves providing students with blank charts and diagrams that they complete as they listen to a discussion or to the teacher's talk. The traditional outline format provides students with a linear overview of material, one that shows a logical sequence of thoughts and that then indicates how details relate to main ideas. However, many times students need to understand how the sequence expressed in the outline was developed, and they need to appreciate that in many instances there is more than one way to organize such a sequence. The following examples of diagrams and charts provide alternatives to the traditional outline format. Also, these formats allow students to begin to assess what is missing from their knowledge base, which is important because, as Glahn (1990) finds, student recognition of their knowledge gaps and their ability to find information to fill them is essential to learning. The following examples are derived from graphic organizers described by McTigue and Lyman (1988) and by Lyman, Lopez, and Mindus (1986). Additional information about graphic organizers and their application to the reading process may be found in Chapter 5.

1. Venn Diagram: This type of chart (Figure 3.4) allows students to list comparisons and contrasts in a visual form. Later, they can organize the information in a variety of ways, depending on their focus or purpose. The example provided here was created by seventh grade students who were discussing, as a prelude to reading a young adult novel from the former Soviet Union, their perceptions of how their lives might be similar to and different from those of their peers who live in Moscow. At the end of the unit, they completed another Venn Diagram, this time to show how their perceptions had changed as a result of reading the text (Stover and Karr 1990).

2. Sequence Chains: This format (Figure 3.5) allows students to keep track of main events that proceed one from the next in a logical sequence, due either to a narrative format or cause/effect connections. To complete the chart, students must determine what events must be represented in the chain, and what information is of a secondary nature, as they move from a starting point to a final end point.

3. Detail Diagrams: Several different formats may prove useful in helping students to collect relevant detail about a topic in an organized fashion. For instance, the "Jellyfish" example in Figure 3.6 shows how an earth science teacher has guided students in organizing the information they garnered while listening to a lecture on "Forces Shaping the Earth." The fact that the three completed boxes entitled "Glaciers—Valley and Continental" "Wind," and "Mass Movement of Surface

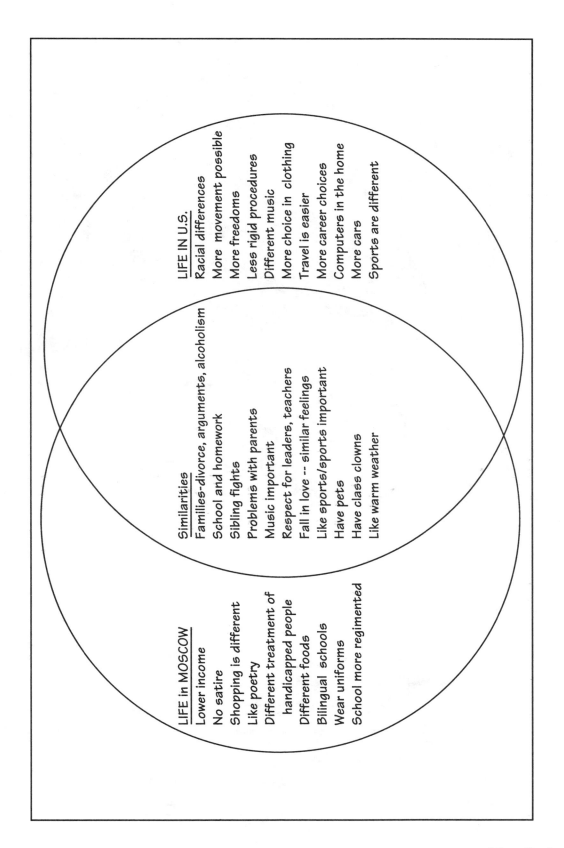

LIFE in MOSCOW
Lower income
No satire
Shopping is different
Like poetry
Different treatment of
   handicapped people
Different foods
Bilingual schools
Wear uniforms
School more regimented

Similarities
Families--divorce, arguments, alcoholism
School and homework
Sibling fights
Problems with parents
Music important
Respect for leaders, teachers
Fall in love -- similar feelings
Like sports/sports important
Have pets
Have class clowns
Like warm weather

LIFE IN U.S.
Racial differences
More movement possible
More freedoms
Less rigid procedures
Different music
More choice in clothing
More career choices
Travel is easier
More career choices
Computers in the home
More cars
Sports are different

Figure 3.4
Seventh Graders' Venn Diagram

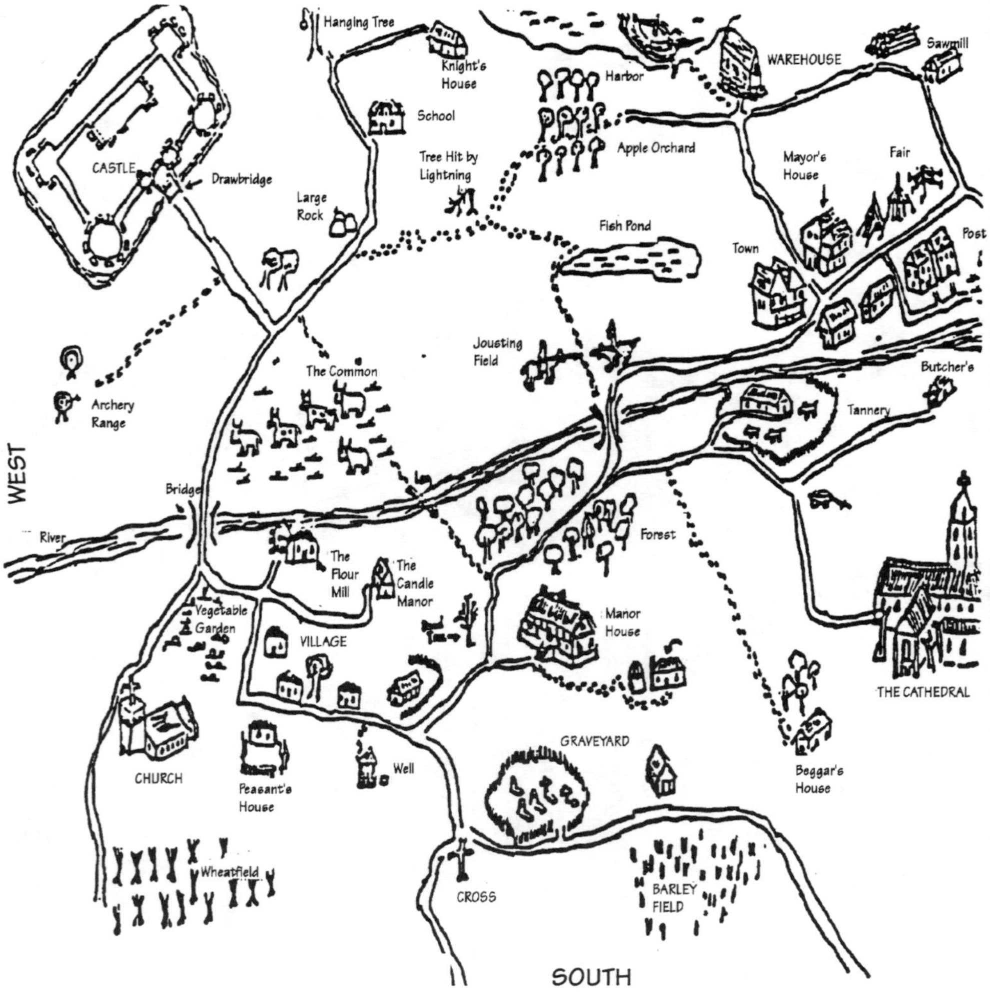

Figure 3.5
Sequence Chains
(Doyle, no date)

Describe how you would get from the CASTLE to a location that is south of the RIVER (Ex. Graveyard). Include directions and name any landmarks that you might pass.

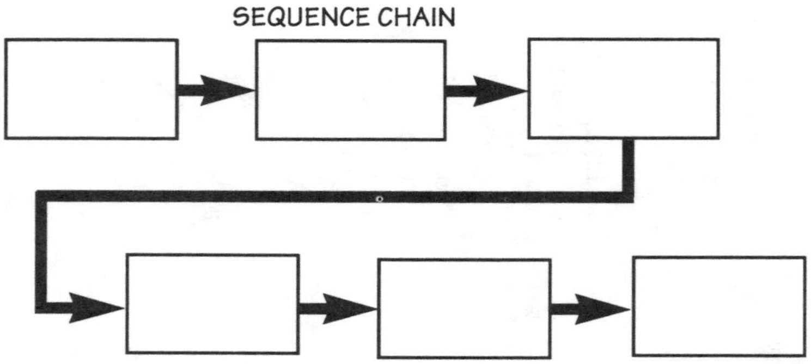

SEQUENCE CHAIN

What application can you think of for using sequence in your subject?

_____
_____
_____
_____
_____

Materials" are situated on the same line visually illustrates that the three forces are of equal importance. In a written essay, it would not matter which topic students chose to discuss first, second, or third.

4. Structured Webs: This format allows the teacher to focus student attention on specific aspects of a topic without restricting the flow of detail that emerges as they brainstorm about it. Once students have offered suggestions for each aspect of the web, the teacher can guide the students as they search for connections and points of overlap. Thus, the students learn that any given detail may be used to support more than one topic sentence, and they begin to understand the recursive nature of thought as it is manifested through speech. The first example offered on page 40 (Figure 3.7), a completed web, illustrates how the web format may be used to collect information about a topic, in this case, "webs." (Doyle). The second example (Figure 3.8) is one students could use to collect information about specific stories (or about an historical concept, such as "revolution;" or a biological concept, such as "cycle"). After completing several such webs, students have a built-in structure to use in comparing and contrasting the stories.

5. Hypothesis-Building Charts: This format (Figure 3.9) allows students to understand how a theory must be supported by facts. The legs of the structure should be completed with facts about the

topic. The facts, when taken together, lead to the generation of an hypothesis. For instance, in a geography class, students could discuss their observations about the relationship between housing structures and climate as they view pictures that illustrate different types of houses from different climates. After they have generated many facts about roof slope, building materials, frequency of windows and other apertures, and so forth, they develop a theory about the relationship. They can test their theory by examining other examples to see whether or not new instances support their original hypothesis or whether the original must be modified in some way (Doyle).

6. Decision-Making Charts: This format may be used to help visualize the decision-making process, based on criteria established by the class. For instance, some students who read the novel *The Chocolate War* by Robert Cormier (1974) were concerned by the fact that the main character, Jerry, made the decisions he did. They brainstormed other possible courses of actions, listed the pros and cons of each one, and determined, in the end, that the novelist's choice for Jerry made sense given his circumstances. A decision-making

chart (Figure 3.10) allowed the students to keep track of their arguments in a visual way so that making a final decision was easier for them to do. Another option for formatting such a chart is to list across the top of the chart specific criteria important to consider when choosing an option.

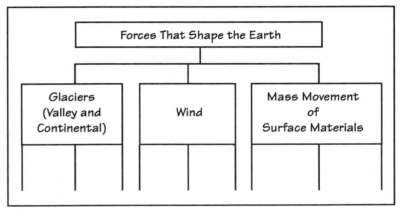

Down the left side, the options are listed. For each option, students consider whether each criteria has been met. When they reach the right-hand column, they add up the number of check marks each option received and thus arrive at the option that is best in a given situation. Figure 3.11 demonstrates how students could use such a chart to decide on a class logo.

Using Visual Reinforcements
Frequently, students fail to process information received through auditory channels because it enters their brains in a sequential way, one word at a time, and they have difficulty translating this linear sequence of words into a coherent whole. Visuals and demonstrations of abstract concepts help

Figure 3.6
Jelly-Fish
Detail Organizer
(Adapted from
Lyman, Lopez, and
Mindus, 1986)

Figure 3.7

Structured Web

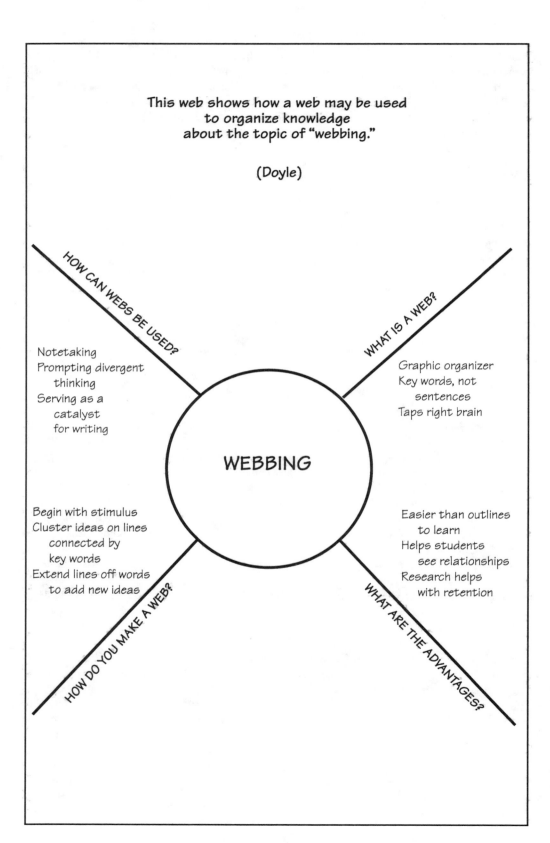

This web shows how a web may be used
to organize knowledge
about the topic of "webbing."

(Doyle)

HOW CAN WEBS BE USED?

Notetaking
Prompting divergent
    thinking
Serving as a
    catalyst
    for writing

WHAT IS A WEB?

Graphic organizer
Key words, not
    sentences
Taps right brain

WEBBING

Begin with stimulus
Cluster ideas on lines
    connected by
    key words
Extend lines off words
    to add new ideas

Easier than outlines
    to learn
Helps students
    see relationships
Research helps
    with retention

HOW DO YOU MAKE A WEB?

WHAT ARE THE ADVANTAGES?

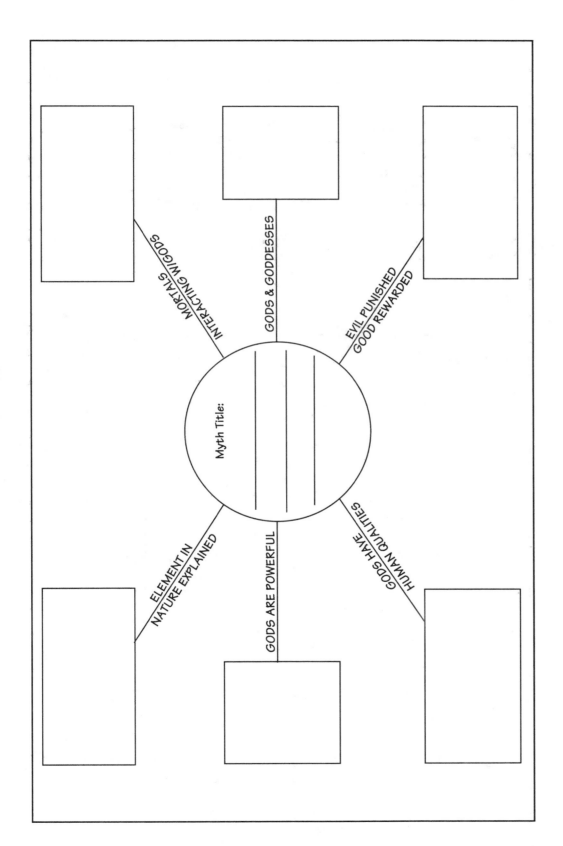

Figure 3.8
Structured Web

Figure 3.9

Hypothesis -

Building

Chart

(Doyle, no date)

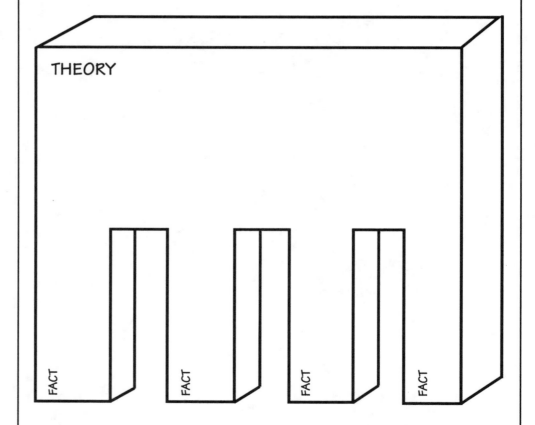

BUILDING A HYPOTHESIS

When students build a hypothesis, they must give a possible
explanation for facts. Pose a problem to a class.
Ask the students to identify the known facts
about the problem on the chart.
Ask them then to write a hypothesis that
helps explain the relationship among the facts.

THEORY

FACT   FACT   FACT   FACT

RELATED WRITING: Ask the students to write to another student
explaining their theory. Have the second student write back responding
to the theory.

students process auditory stimuli more effectively. For instance, it is difficult to listen to a lecture about Sherman's march to Atlanta without being able to see the route traced on a map. And watching the health teacher manipulate the bones on a model skeleton helps students understand how those bones relate in a way that just hearing about them does not. Any time the teacher can show material as well as talk about it, students should learn more effectively because that information is going into their brains through more than one channel. The visual input allows students to create concrete images of concepts or information that may be abstract when presented only in auditory form. But it is also important to recognize that material delivered primarily through a visual or kinesthetic mode requires a verbal explanation. Read the following brief descriptions of lessons centered around lectures, lecture/demonstrations, and field trips and consider how the visual input might be enhanced by verbal input.

1. A physics teacher might engender students' interest in the properties of waves by using a demonstration that shows waves in motion and then provides visual information about what happens when an obstruction is placed in the path of the wave or what happens when an alternate force is applied.

2. An art teacher might model for students how to use the brush technique of stippling in the context of a painting to create a desired effect.

3. An English teacher might show the class his or her own "cut and paste" efforts in revising an essay on the computer. It is difficult to imagine learning how to use a computer without being able to watch—and, ideally, to try—the machine being used.

4. Biology students on a field trip to a local bird sanctuary will hear the birds, hear a park ranger or ornithologist talking about the birds, and see the birds and their habitat all at once.

5. Students in an Algebra II class who visit the offices of an insurance company will see actuaries using statistical information to predict life expectancies and create insurance rate charts as they hear from these professionals about the challenges of the job and about the use of probability formulas in their daily lives.

We have discussed why visual input is an important supplement to auditory input. Now, why, when a teacher provides strong visual input, is the auditory information that frequently accompanies it so important? Most significantly, the verbal information clarifies and organizes the visual. By describing what the students see, or by asking questions to help them make sense of their visual intake, teachers help students attend to those aspects of the demonstration that are most important or most relevant to their own future use of the information. For the unskilled, inexperienced physics student observing the wave demonstration, it is difficult to know to what aspects of the demonstration to attend. With the addition of teacher talk, the student's viewing is focused and guided so that he or she may be able to generalize and hypothesize.

Encouraging Active Listening

Many texts for future teachers define *active listening* fairly narrowly, using the term in the context of a discussion of classroom-management techniques as an example of a strategy to try when students are upset or unhappy (Ginott 1972). In such situations, the teacher's job is to reflect back to the student what the student has said for the purpose of letting the student know that he or she has been attended to, that his or her message has been received. Students can be called upon to be active listeners in this sense as a first step in developing the habit of active listening by teachers who sys-

A. Jerry's Possible Courses of Action When Faced with Vigils' "Assignment"	Pros	Cons
1. Tell father.		
2. Seek advice from sympathetic teacher.		
3. Organize peers.		
4. Ask to change schools.		
5. Agree to assignment.		
6. Etc.		

Figure 3.10
Decision-Making
Chart I
(Adapted from
Lyman, Lopez, and
Mindus, 1986)

tematically ask students to paraphrase, either verbally or in writing, what they hear, whether they are listening to the teacher or a peer. If stu-

Class Logo	CRITERIA					Total Points
	Includes Whole Class in Description	Slogan Easy to Say	Visual Is Eye-Catching	Visual and Verbal Blend Well	Easy to Reproduce	
1. Group One	X	X	X	X		(4)
2. Group Two		X			X	2
3. Group Three	X		X		X	3
4. Group Four		X	X	X		3

Figure 3.11

Decision-Making

Chart II

dents can reflect, to the speaker's satisfaction, the gist of the spoken text, they have a useful starting point for manipulating the information in that text in other situations. When a discussion of a controversial topic is becoming heated, for instance, it can be useful to insist that speakers paraphrase the preceding speaker's thoughts to that person's satisfaction before offering their own. In this way, problems that arise over semantic issues can often be avoided, and students often find that they are more in tune with each other's points of view than they had thought.

If students perceive that their comments are not truly heard, they stop wanting to contribute their own ideas and seek, instead, to guess what the teacher has in mind. Thus,

during a class discussion, when the teacher writes student comments on the board, he or she should ask students if the paraphrase the teacher has generated accurately reflects the student's point of view. The teacher can also model asking probing questions as a strategy for clarifying a particular point, can model the active listening strategy of reflecting back to the student the emotional gist of what the student has offered, and can encourage students to do the same for each other. Dillon (1984) outlined seven possible strategies, each representative of "active listening," useful in responding to student discourse without asking questions.

1. Avoid "message overload." Do not deliver too much information verbally at any given point in time.

2. Attend to all the factors that can inhibit effective listening. Create a positive environment for listening free of external noise.

3. Help students check out their biases and assumptions, which may interfere with their ability to listen.

4. Teach listening skills directly.

5. Model effective listening techniques yourself. Be an "active listener" by "listening between the lines" and by avoiding "tuning out" what

students are saying (Vining and Yrle, 1980).

6. Reward students for being good listeners.

Pogonowski (1989) has provided the following examples of active listening statements made by the teacher and students in an actual music lesson.

1. **Declarative Statement:** "I think your case for calling this piece a Baroque composition based on the use of fugal procedures is fine. We do know, however, that Mozart, Berlioz, and Brahms, among others, include these procedures in their works."

2. **Reflective Statement:** "I understand you to mean that because certain Baroque characteristics occur in this work, we can take the entire work as such."

3. **Description of Listener's State of Mind:** "I'm sorry, I didn't quite get your point."

4. **Invitations to Elaboration:** "I'd like to hear more of your views."

5. **Encouragement of Speaker to Question Self:** "John, can you think of any arguments against your proposal?"

6. **Encouragement of Other Listeners to Question Speaker:** "Sarah, how do you feel about the point Jane is making?"

7. **Maintenance of Deliberate, Appreciative Silence:** The teacher counts to 60 before reiterating a question, or the teacher enforces a minute of silent reflection or free-writing before allowing any student to respond to a question or another student's

comments.

SUMMARY

Drawing on what we know about the nature of the listening process and the characteristics of effective listeners, teachers who seek to create an interactive classroom environment should encourage students, through the use of teacher- and self-questioning to check the accuracy of what they hear and to determine its significance as they seek to integrate new information into an existing scaffold on knowledge or ideas. In interactive classrooms, teachers help students to articulate the assumptions about themselves and their world that may affect their ability to attend to auditory information or that may distort it as they encode it and store it in those existing mental compartments.

Teachers eager to help their students develop as listeners recognize students' inclination to be egocentric and preoccupied with self, and they build on this self-interest by creating verbal analogies between content and "real life" as they tap prior experience before asking students to listen. And, in interactive classrooms, teachers help motivate their students to listen by providing a purpose for listening. Teachers who attend to the development of their students' listening skills by asking questions, guiding reflection, guiding attention through the use of graphic organizers, using visual reinforcement, and active listening have students who are rewarded for their listening skill because they perform better when called upon to use the knowledge gained through listening. That knowledge is more accurate, more organized, and therefore more retrievable, than that of their peers who do not listen well.

We should not assume that all students are listening effectively, and we should not leave the development of these skills to chance. Using the strategies outlined for preparing students to listen and for enhancing their listening when we use teaching techniques such as lectures, demonstrations, audiovisual aids, role play, and discussions should help students both learn the content of our lessons more effectively and develop the listening skills they will need for success outside the classroom at the same time.

BIBLIOGRAPHY

- Abrell, R. "Preventing Communications Breakdowns." *NASSP Bulletin* 68 (1984): 97–104.
- Adler, R.B., and Towne, N. *Looking Out/Looking In*, fifth edition. New York: Holt, Rinehart, and Winston, 1987.
- Ausabel, D. "The Advanced Organizer Model." In *Models of Teaching*, B. Joyce and M. Weil, eds., second edition. Englewood Cliffs, N.J.: Prentice-Hall, 1980.
- Bradley, B.E. *Fundamentals of Speech Communication*, sixth edition. Dubuque, Iowa: W.C. Brown, 1991.
- Cormier, R. *The Chocolate War*. New York: Dell, 1974.
- Devine, T. "Listening: What Do We Know After 50 Years of Research and Theorization?" *Journal of Reading* 21 (1978): 296–304.
- Dillon, J.T. "Research on Questions and Discussions." *Educational Leadership* 42 (1984): 50–56.
- Doyle, R. "Webbing as Prewriting Strategy." Baltimore: Maryland Writing Project, Towson State University, n.d. (photocopy).
- Forster, P., and Doyle, B.A. "Teaching Listening Skills to Students with Attention Deficit Disorders." *Teaching Exceptional Children* 21 (1989): 21–22.
- Glahn, E. "On the Pedagogical and Technological Development of a Computer-Assisted Exercise in Listening Comprehension." 1990. [ED 323 803]
- Gleason, M.M., and others. "Study Skills." *Teaching Exceptional Children* 20 (1988): 52–57.
- Ginott, H. *Teacher and Child*. New York: Avon, 1972.
- Grandegenett, D. "Help Your Students Build Effective Listening Skills." *Social Studies Teacher* 4 (1987): 3,6.
- Hinds, A., and Pankake, A.. "Listening: The Missing Side of School Communication." *Clearing House* 60 (1987): 281–83.
- Joiner, E., Adkins, P.B., and Eykyn, L.B. "Skimming and Scanning with Champs-Elysees: Using Authentic Materials to Improve Foreign Language Listening." *French Review* 62 (1989): 427–35.
- Langan, J. *Reading and Study Skills, Form B*. New York: McGraw-Hill, 1987.
- Lyman, F. "The Responsive Classroom Discussion: The Inclusion of All Students." *Mainstreaming Digest*, University of Maryland (1981): 109–12.
- Lyman, F., Lopez, C., and Mindus, A. "Think-Links: The Shaping of Thought in Response to Reading." Unpublished manuscript, Columbia, Md. 1986.

- McTighe, J., and Lyman, F. "Cuing Thinking in the Classroom: The Promise of Theory-Embedded Tools." *Educational Leadership* 45 no. 7 (1988): 18–24.

- Neil, F. "Everybody's Talkin." Third Story Music, copyright 1967.

- Nelson, D., and Heeney, W. "Directed Listening: A Model for Improved Administrative Communication." *NASSP Bulletin* 68 (1984): 124–29.

- Nichols, J. "Using Paragraph Frames to Help Remedial High School Students with Written Assignments." *Journal of Reading* 24 (1980): 228–31.

- Nichols, R.G. "Listening as a Ten-Part Skill." In *Readings in Interpersonal and Organizational Communication*, R. Huseman, C. Logue, and D. Freshley, eds., third edition. Boston: Holbrook Press, 1977.

- Pauk, W. *How to Study in College.* Boston: Houghton Mifflin, 1984.

- Pogonowski, L. "Critical Thinking and Music Listening." *Music Educators Journal* 76 (1989): 35–38.

- Reetz, L., and Hoover, J. *Secondary LD Mainstreaming Methods: Instructional Module.* ERIC Document ED 3181461, 1989.

- Stover, L. "Exploring and Celebrating Cultural Similarities and Differences Through Young Adult Literature." *The ALAN Review* 18 (1991): 12–16.

- Stover, L., and Karr, R. "Glasnost in the Classroom." *English Journal* 79 (1990): 47–53.

- Verderber, R., and Verderber, K. *Inter-Act: Using Interpersonal Communication Skill*, fifth edition. Belmont, Calif.: Wadsworth Publishing, 1986.

- Vining, J.W., and Yrle, A.C. "How Do You Rate as a Listener?" *Supervisory Management* 25 (1980): 22–25.

PRACTICE

1. As you sit in a classroom this week, make a record of who is speaking and who is listening, and to whom, during five-minute intervals. What generalizations can you make about the quality of engagement through listening that you observed or experienced in this class?

2. Think about a class you observed this week. Free-write about whether or not you were actively engaged in the learning process as a listener, and discuss what the teacher or students could have done to foster mental engagement of the students by consciously guiding their listening.

3. Go back to Ms. Jones's lesson in Chapter 1. Make a list of times when she expected the students to be learning primarily through the act of listening. Pick three of these and describe how she could revise her instruction to better encourage active listening on the part of the students.

4. Consider a teacher you have observed teaching on at least five occasions. Free-write about how that teacher does or does not model the art of active listening, and describe the effect you believe the teacher's listening behavior has on the listening and speaking behavior of the students.

5. Write out at least three goals for yourself as a teacher who hopes to maximize your students' abilities to be actively involved in the learning process through the act of listening.

6. Plan a lesson centered about the use of any of the following strategies: lecture or lecture/demonstration, field trips, audiovisual aids, role play, small or large group discussion. Consider the following questions as you plan.

   • When is this strategy (i.e., a lecture) a useful and appropriate strategy?

   • What are my objectives for this lesson, and is this strategy the best way to accomplish those objectives?

   • What strategies might I use to gain students' attention before beginning the lesson and asking them to listen?

   • What strategies might be useful in purpose setting prior to asking students to listen?

   • What strategies might I use during the course of this lesson to ensure that students are continuing to listen and to determine whether or not they are processing the information appropriately?

   • How can I engage students in processing the information they have received once the lesson is over?

CLASSROOM CARRY-OVER

Here's how I can use what I learned about listening in the interactive classroom.

_____
_____
_____
_____
_____
_____
_____
_____
_____
_____
_____
_____
_____
_____
_____
_____
_____
_____
_____
_____
_____
_____
_____
_____
_____
_____
_____
_____
_____
_____
_____
_____
_____

CHAPTER 4

Speaking in the Interactive Classroom

How do you use speaking activities to enhance learning?

READINESS

Picture yourself in an introductory methodology course or an inservice course. Your instructor has organized the class into groups of five, asking each to develop a definition of the word *profession* and a set of defining characteristics that separate professions from non-professions. After several minutes of reflection and individual note taking, your group eagerly begins to share ideas and work toward consensus. Your teacher suddenly interrupts and asks each group to select one member to serve as recorder who should be prepared to summarize the group's key ideas afterward. So, who will it be? Doreen (sitting next to you) immediately says, "No way; not me!" Darrell casts his eyes down at the table. He wants out. Bob's body language implies the same. He says nothing. Francine looks imploringly at you and indicates she hates to get up in front of people; besides, she says you are good at this sort of thing. Naturally, all the others agree! Guess you are stuck—again!

Sound familiar? Why is it some students are reluctant to speak in front of their peers? What causes this reticence?

How would you like to be the person who is "stuck" with the responsibility of recorder? Assume this has happened previously in this teacher's class. If you were the teacher, how might you organize this activity differently? What value do speakers derive that nonspeakers do not? How can the teacher involve all students in diverse speaking opportunities, both informal and formal, so that all individuals in the class use the speaking process to enhance their understanding of content, to construct new knowledge, and to develop speaking skills?

Purpose for Reading

This reading will attempt to answer the following questions.

1. What is the speaking process, and what does theory and research tell us about the value of speech-communication skills in secondary school classrooms?

2. How do speaking skills relate to active learning?

3. What special teaching strategies can teachers use to facilitate students' comprehension of the course material, to manipulate and extend that knowledge base, and to invite social interaction?

READING MATERIAL

This section takes a comprehensive look at the speaking process and its relationship to learning.

The Speaking Process And the Value of Speaking to Learn

Think back to your experience as a student during those middle school and high school years. With a partner, discuss how active or passive your classes were. Who talked the most—students or teachers? How involved were you? Your classmates? Did you speak frequently? Why? Why not? Do you feel you made a worthwhile contribution to your classes, or were you largely uninvolved? What benefits did you derive from verbal participation in class?

Students who are products of teacher-centered, passive classrooms are not likely to have frequent opportunities to contribute meaningfully in class—to ask cogent questions, participate in group discussions, role-play in front of peers, or present oral reports to the class. The use of language, however, is essential to individual growth and to social communication.

Milner and Milner (1993)

describe four foundational assumptions about learning and language.

- Learning is social and is constructed by the action of learners in interaction with their environment and others.
- Learning develops gradually over time according to a developmental sequence that moves from the simple to the complex, from the concrete to the abstract.
- Learning is not linear (moving in a straight line along a single dimension), but recursive (circling, repeating along complex dimensions).
- Language learning develops through a never-ending process, and that process, not the product of it, should be our instructional focus.

Active language production—in this case, speech—is developed in classrooms where teachers provide constant opportunities for students to interact verbally. Moffett and Wagner (1992) observed that:

> Because constant practice and good interaction are the best teachers of speaking and listening, talk in small groups should be a staple learning activity for all grades and allotted a large amount of time in the curriculum.

Through speaking, students learn social interaction skills, become active participants, and build self-esteem.

They also develop understandings, analyze critically, make judgments, and learn to think and express themselves clearly (Phelan 1989; Mahood, Biemer, and Lowe 1991).

What is Speaking?

Speech is the communication of thought and emotion by means of voice, language, and/or bodily action (Dickens 1973). For students, speech may take the form of responding to or asking questions, discussion, oral presentations, interactions in groups, reading aloud, acting, or simple conversation.

Five Essential Components In the Speech-Communication Process

At its most basic level, the speech-communication process involves a communicator who encodes a message (words, gestures, or physical experiences, such as role playing or dramatics) that is sent to a receiver who decodes the message (either internally as thought or in the form of a verbal or nonverbal response). Speech involves the use of language or codes, for example, vocabulary, semantics, syntax, idioms, and slang. These codes influence the nature of the message. Both the communicator and the receiver possess cognitive structures consisting of prior knowledge, values, attitudes, beliefs, prejudices, and skills. These structures affect which messages are sent, the intent of the messages, and the response to messages received. A final element in the speech process is feedback—the receiver's response, whether verbal or nonverbal—illustrating the ongoing nature of the speech-communication process (Faust and McGlone 1972, Gronbeck 1979). (See Figure 4.1.)

It is important to understand that speech is also affected by where it takes place—by its context. Shouting "fire" on a pistol range evokes an entirely different reaction than a student shouting "fire" in a crowded school cafeteria. Similarly, messages have different meaning, given the culture or society in which delivered. For example, haggling over the price of a tee shirt at Macy's Department Store is unheard of, but it is expected at a bazaar in Egypt.

Context and culture are important variables in the speech process as messages are given, received, and responded to in the classroom. A school-related example of context and culture might be illustrated by a white teacher teaching a class of predominately minority students (African-American, Hispanic, Asian, or a mixture of these) where frequent use is made of "street language" and where cultural heritage affects the way students interact with others (e.g., "high fives," vocal affirmations, voice inflections). For a teacher to really understand the intent of the message, he or she needs to understand the context and cultural background in which the message has its origins.

In describing the process of speaking, Supreme Court Justice Robert H. Jackson made this observation:

I used to say that, as Solicitor General, I made three arguments of every case. First came the one that I planned—as I thought—logical, coherent, complete. Second was the one actually presented—interrupted, incoherent, disjointed, disappointing. The third was the utterly devastating argument that I thought of after going to bed that night (Jackson 1951).

What elements of the speech-communication process are suggested in Justice Jackson's observation? The first point Justice Jackson makes is that planning what one wants to say is important. Next comes delivery or presentation. Finally, there is the evaluation stage, where the speaker evaluates what has occurred and plans his or her next move. Speaking, whether in a court of law or in a secondary school classroom, is an important learning process, where speakers state ideas and clarify their perceptions, thereby increasing their knowledge, attitudes, and skills.

Return to Mr. Smith's Lesson in Chapter 1. With a partner, first discuss and then create a list of at least three opportunities students had to use speech interaction as a means of developing a better understanding of the lesson content. Have any difficulty? Probably not; Mr. Smith has students actively engaged in the speaking process throughout the lesson.

He calls on students to process the free-writing activity at the outset of class. Next, he asks students to relate the free-writing activity to their study of the colonial period. Later, he has students work in pairs, calling on pairs to help build a master chart on the chalkboard. After breaking the class into two groups, he has each group create lists of reasons to defend its position on separation from the mother country. After organizing their notes, students share what they have written with a nearby classmate, and then Mr. Smith has the class volunteer some responses to a fill-in-the-blank statement. At the lesson's end, Mr. Smith asks students to respond to his closing, predictive question. This lesson has frequent opportunities for students to be engaged in the speaking process, where they demonstrate understanding of lesson content and construct new knowledge about events that led to the American Revolution.

What Students Do When Speaking

Return to the "Readiness" scenario on the word *profession* at the beginning of this chapter. If it is *you* who must speak in front of your classmates, what is it you need to do, and how does this relate to the five components of the speech-communication process?

Because your task is to record and summarize, you will need to be an attentive listener and an accurate note taker. You will also need to ask group members to clarify key ideas, making sure to succinctly express their points of view—particularly contrasting or divergent ideas. Don't

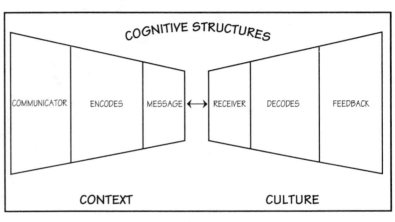

forget to express your own views, too! As discussion reaches closure, you will want to verbalize your understanding of the group's definition of *profession* and its defining characteristics, making certain your "sense of the group" is validated by others. This gives you important feedback on your own thinking process. All of this is done through discussion—speaking with fellow group members. The final step is presenting to the entire class (i.e., externalizing the thoughts of the group by passing them through your own linguistic network in language that makes sense to you and is confirmed by members of your group). To make all this happen, your ideas need to be organized and clearly and succinctly stated.

Figure 4.1
The Speech Communication Process

How does what you have just done relate to the five components of the speech-communication process? As communicator you have a message to deliver. To deliver a clear, accurate, and succinct message, you will have to encode it properly so that it reflects the sense of the group rather than your own thinking/bias. Your message will be heard by many receivers (fellow students and the teacher) who will decode it, giving it special meaning, depending upon the cognitive structures, context, and cultural influences that impact upon them. Their feedback will be received by you, decoded (passed through your cognitive structures, context, and cultural influences) and form the basis of a reaction (follow-up message), should you feel the need or be required to do so by the teacher.

As you can see, much is involved in the simple task of presenting a few ideas to the class. Presenting ideas effectively is much more than just "winging it." As Justice Jackson intimated, there is much complexity to the planning and delivery of speech communication and both joy and anxiety connected with the feedback/evaluation given by others and rendered by yourself. No wonder some students avoid speaking responsibilities. Not only does this task involve using effective presentation skills before the entire class, but it also requires effective interpersonal communication skills necessary to be a good clarifier, discussant, and sum-

marizer. These skills do not "just occur" in the educational process; they need to be expressly provided by teachers (Chapin and Gross 1973).

In order to speak, students must think. Speaking, whether extemporaneous or planned, offers students opportunities to *construct knowledge* for themselves. They search through their cognitive structures, actively retrieving and working on prior knowledge to shape it into a new, meaningful whole (Neubert and Binka 1992). Students must *act upon* knowledge for it to move from short-term memory into long-term memory. The deeper the processing, the better it is stored in long-term memory and the more easily it is retrieved (Myers and Myers 1990). Discussions, oral presentations, role playings, and questioning sessions, provide these opportunities for students to *process* what they are learning. Memorization and paraphrasing of concepts without understanding them is mere "verbalism" and a "waste of time and energy for all involved" (Tonjes and Zintz 1992).

Speaking Opportunities In the Classroom

There is a wide range of speaking opportunities teachers can use to change the character of their classrooms, making them active learning environments where students take increased responsibility for their learning and where the teacher functions as a guide and facilitator in the learning process. Chief among these are the use of groups.

First we will examine a rationale for using entire class grouping. Then we will focus on collaborative strategies and, next, we will discuss cooperative learning strategies in which students not only develop knowledge but practice socialization skills in a guided, deliberate fashion. Finally, we will explore individual speaking opportunities.

Rationale for Whole-Class Grouping vs. Small Groups
Teachers need to consider carefully how best to format class-speaking activities designed to help students construct knowledge. There are three basic configurations that foster student-speaking skills: whole-class grouping, collaborative small groups, and opportunities where individuals are in the limelight. Whole-class activities provide excellent opportunities for students to verbalize thinking. Here, the larger class size does not impede thinking and can actually enhance it, as with group brainstorming, processing drills, whole-class reviews, recall activities, and discussions based on widespread pupil participation.

Certain class activities, especially in-depth discussions, need to be conducted in small groups for students to be meaningfully engaged in thinking and speaking. Among the most effective small group techniques are small work groups and cooperative learning groups. In this setting student interaction and cooperation contribute to improved problem solving; increased achievement; better retention of material; and better attitudes toward school, subject, teachers, and peers (Lyman and Foyle 1990).

Some activities are best suited to individual students working on their own, whether it be processing drills, seatwork in class, responding to teacher questions, or oral presentations before small groups or the entire class.

The teacher's task is to decide which strategy—whole class, small group, or individual—best suits the purpose. If the aim is to prompt students to think and learn through interactive speaking, a classroom setting that best facilitates this objective is needed. For example, a teacher might ask the class to generate ideas for a field trip or perhaps to speculate about the President of the United States' foreign policy agenda. Both of these activities are well suited to a whole-class discussion. If, however, students were examining aspects of Africa in detail, the teacher might have small groups investigate African history, economic development, customs and traditions in various geographic areas, independence movements, and health issues. Each of these topics would require small groups that would report back to the class at a later time. This "Africa" activity would not work well in an entire class setting. If an art teacher wanted to target individual speaking opportunities to enhance class learning, he or she might require each class member to provide a brief analysis of an impressionist painting so that the class, as a whole, develops a knowledge of 25 works, while individuals hone their understanding of impressionism through concentrated investigation and class sharing.

Whole-Class Discussions

Recall discussions in which you participated as a college student. List specific strategies your teachers employed to facilitate effective whole-class discussions and effective small group discussions. Compare your list with a classmate's. What additional strategies have you learned from your classmate? Add these to your original list. Now, compare your master list with the following suggestions for organizing entire class and small group discussions.

The most widely used form of discussion is that conducted with the entire class. Because teachers frequently engage in entire class discussions, they should employ strategies designed to foster student interaction and build effective speaking skills.

- **Seating Arrangements:** Organize the classroom in a manner that facilitates the exchange of views. Traditional row-upon-row seating often inhibits class discussion (although it may be necessary for a variety of reasons, including the fact that some classes need a great deal of structure). Just as in real life, it is more motivating and easier to speak to someone with whom one can make eye contact. Therefore, always consider using worktables, desk clusters, theater-style seating, fishbowls, United Nations forums, and other interactive settings to increase the potential for the exchange of ideas between students and teachers. If the classroom has individual desks, not fixed to the floor, desk clusters may be one of the best approaches. Using clusters, the classroom can be arranged and rearranged quickly and easily, especially if another teacher uses the room the following class period.
- **Student Participation:** Call on a wide range of students, asking for additional examples, further clarification, more information, other ideas, and views. Encourage students to volunteer and provide a class atmosphere that invites students to participate and one in which it is "OK" to have an incorrect answer. How does Mr. Smith solicit responses from students? Did you note his frequent use of student pairs and small groups? These facilitate student interaction and make it safe for students to respond.
- **Background:** Students can not discuss a topic they know nothing about Make certain the class

has the appropriate information background to provide a starting point for increasing knowledge and for supporting discussion. Sampling student-background knowledge is often helpful, but often serves more as a starting point for learning than an ending point. Brainstorming is also useful for generating a variety of ideas that can serve as springboard for discussion. However, if teachers wish students to discuss in-depth, then they must make certain students have sufficient specific information to discuss in detail (information either introduced by them—i.e., through text, lecture, film, video—or generated by students through research, investigation, or direct experience).

- **Conversation Flow:** Develop a procedure for giving students the opportunity to contribute. Have them raise hands, interrupt politely when another finishes speaking, or address the teacher as the person managing the class discussion. You might also help students learn appropriate ways to interject thoughts when someone else has the floor (polite "butting in"). A laudable goal is to work toward students learning to freely interact among themselves without restrictive rules. Gen-

erally, teachers find that when discussions proceed smoothly, the need for rules often disappears.

- **Addressing Comments:** Ask students to address their comments to the class as well as to the teacher. Try to shift the focus of the discussion to the class and away from the teacher (What do they think? What alternatives would they offer? How do they feel about what another student said, etc.?). Be a facilitator not a controller. Encourage students to address each other by using first names. Discussions lend themselves to personalization, not formality.

- **Clarity:** Have students speak clearly, distinctly, and sufficiently loud to be heard by all in the classroom. Many discussions have been ruined by the inability of participants to hear. Student interest falls off rapidly and the quality of the discussion declines. It is the teacher's responsibility to gently yet firmly insist that students speak up and also speak clearly and distinctly.

- **Language Usage:** Help students to understand the difference between the appropriate use of formal language in a classroom discussion and of informal language when talking socially or communicating with friends.

- **Higher Level Thinking:** Challenge student thinking by asking higher level questions. The more teachers require students to think, the more that reflective disposition is fostered, which ultimately will lead them to challenge others to think. Use questions such as the following.
  1. Why do you think that is so?
  2. What reasons can you give to support that conclusion?
  3. What evidence can you cite to support the position taken?
  4. What conclusions might we draw from that data?
  5. Is there any sign of bias in the author's statement?
  6. What assumptions are apparent?
  7. How do you know this is the right answer?

- **Elaboration:** Have students elaborate and clarify whenever appropriate. Don't be too eager to accept "yes/no" or simplistic answers.

- **Politeness and Consideration:** Encourage this behavior from all participants.

Collaborative Small Groups
Small groups in which students collaborate together to construct new knowledge for themselves and clarify existing knowledge through verbal interaction are central to the functioning of interactive

classrooms (see Chapter 3). These collaborative small groups take many forms and most present excellent opportunities for developing students' speaking and group-socialization skills. Among the most popular forms of collaborative small groups are those for which the constituency is based on reading level or on student interest and need for accomplishing tutorial work. Small groups, including dyads (such as Think/Pair/Share) and triads, can be created so that students work together to conduct discussions, research, or peer review of classwork. See Figure 4.2 for a listing of types of collaborative small groups and a description of their purposes (Shepherd 1972).

Unlike entire class discussions where teachers exercise extensive control, some collaborative small groups require a greater amount of advance teacher planning, organization, and direction because students are working on their own. Other small groups place students in situations where the level of difficulty does not require teacher monitoring and where students can and should carry out tasks on their own. Collaborative groups also require students to exercise appropriate self-control and on-task behavior. When students lack these skills, teachers should have them work as partners for limited periods of time, building their social skills to the point where more involved, larger group work is possible. ("Success breeds success!")

As teachers plan for collaborative small groups, they should keep in mind the following suggestions to help students be effective when working together and presenting before the class.

- **Topics:** Make certain that discussion topics have a direct relationship to the curriculum and relevance to the lives of students. This helps to ensure student interest and build motivation for successful student engagement. In such activities, students need to "connect" to the topic. For example, at the outset of this chapter, you were asked to think about and discuss with a partner your experiences as a participant in whole class and small group discussions. This was done to motivate your willingness to read this chapter and to activate your prior cognitive structures.

- **Focusing Questions:** Students need direction in the form of questions to help provide focus to the discussion. Discussion need not be limited to teacher questions, but these questions are important for getting things started and ensuring a focus consistent with lesson objectives. Most often the teacher provides these focusing questions. At other times, students can (and should!) generate them.

- **Room Setup:** Traditional row-upon-row seating does not facilitate the exchange of views, which is necessary in small group work. Worktables, desk clusters, theater-style seating, fishbowls, United

Type of Group	Purpose
Reading Level	Provides content study at different reading levels so that every student can succeed
Need	Gives specific instruction for an observed skill deficiency
Research	Supplements basic textbook materials
Interest	Expands student interest through opportunity to investigate additional information
Social	Allows students to work on specific topics with peers of their choice
Guidance	Allows disparate students to work together in order to foster greater social development and tolerance
Dyad or Triad	Has two or three students work on a problem to mutual advantage of each
Tutorial	Pairs student who needs intensive help because of lack of competence or has a special skill need with a student who has expertise in that area
Personality	Matches students with similar personalities to avoid conflicts and maximize group productivity

Adapted from Shepherd, David L. *Comprehensive High School Reading Methods.* Columbus: Charles Merrill, 1972.

Figure 4.2

Forms of Grouping

Nations forums, and other interactive settings increase student-speaking potential and the opportunity for students to plan and work closely together. Group size is also important. The smaller the group, the easier it is to speak freely (Chapin and Gross 1973). And the smaller the group, the more difficult it is to "hide" and avoid making contributions. Depending upon purpose, two to 10 members appear to be most effective.

- **Roles**: Help students to learn the various roles they can play in groups (e.g., leader/chair, recorder, reporter, timekeeper, first speaker, second speaker, summarizer). Give them specific practice in these roles.

- **Group Constituency**: A heterogeneous grouping constituency appears to be most effective for small groups (Staton 1983, Johnson et. al. 1984). For instance, an English teacher might group and regroup, depending on the lesson objectives, to balance ability, achievement, interest, learning styles, cultural background and race, gender, and personality style. The tutorial aspect of groups maximizes opportunities for higher order thinking and social interaction. For example, an English teacher might group students by learning styles, with visual learners in one group, so that they can create/review materials best suited for their need for visuals. At other times, that same teacher might create groups for peer-editing sessions, mixing students with strong punctuation skills, students strong in spelling ability, and students strong in vocabulary use. There are, however, occasions when teachers might allow some classes to self-select groups. The most important consideration for the teacher is what group constituency will best maximize appropriate student interaction consistent with lesson objectives.

- **Planning, Preparation, and Directions**: Some collaborative small group tasks need require little in the way of student advance planning, perhaps only a brief amount of time to read background material. Others require a good deal of research and processing by group members before the general discussion or group presentation takes place. Often the teacher needs to provide clear directions, structuring for reading and content investigation, group subtasks, discussion questions, and/or criteria for oral presentations. Failure to provide clear directions may result in chaos. At times specific suggestions need to be given regarding how students might organize their groups (specific roles, subdivision of tasks), yet at other times these decisions can be left to the students (maturity and skill level are two important considerations). Be sure to give sufficient time for planning, preparation, and presentation of group efforts. If the activity is worth doing, it is worth doing right!

- **Feedback/Evaluation and Monitoring**: Unless students receive practice and frank feedback on their progress as participants in small group activities, they are not likely to improve their skills. Some popular feedback and evaluation strategies used by teachers follow.
  1. Written evaluations
  2. Checklists or rating sheets by group members (See Figure 4.3.)
  3. Tapes (audio and/or video)
  4. Individual personal comments by teacher

Teachers need to monitor discussions to determine whether or not the group is "on task" and how to adjust time before shifting to the next activity. Failure to monitor the discussion may undo all the hard work of both teachers and students.

What Are Cooperative Learning Groups?
The most often talked about and researched teaching tool

A rating sheet, based upon the objectives previously agreed upon, often helps each group diagnose its own difficulties and evaluate its own accomplishments. The same holds true for the individual. The first two forms may prove useful with beginners.

GROUP'S SELF-RATING

Purpose: _____

1. Did we get to work promptly?   4.   Did all contribute?
2. Did we stick to the point?   5.   Did we ask for help as soon as we needed it?
3. Did we work quietly?   What did we accomplish? _____

Such a reaction sheet, completed by the group, serves as impetus for a class evaluation that re-emphasizes the purpose of the experience and the means used for its accomplishment.

BEGINNER'S CHECKLIST FOR SELF-RATING

Subject: _____

1. Did I prepare sufficiently?   4.   Did I work without disturbing other groups?
2. Did I follow directions?   5.   My chief contribution to my group was:
3. Did I make the best use of my time?   _____

After several meetings, let students draw names to rate one other member.

EVALUATION OF A GROUP MEMBER

1. What was his or her chief contribution?
2. What factor should he or she first try to improve?
3. Evaluation by: _____

With an experienced group, a more complete rating is possible. In developing a form, select only times in which instruction has been given and ask the student to select several aspects of his or her performance to evaluate in a brief essay.

CHECKLIST FOR SELF-RATING BY MORE MATURE STUDENTS

1. Did I assume the responsibility the group wished?
2.   Did I listen alertly?
3. Did I willingly express my own point of view?
4. Did I try to understand the viewpoint of others?
5. Did I attempt to assess the strengths and weaknesses of all opinions expressed?
6   Did I encourage those who seemed reluctant to speak?
7. Did I help the chairperson maintain a friendly, businesslike atmosphere?
8. Did I keep the discussion moving purposefully?
9. Did I subordinate my own wishes to further the aim of the group?
10. My greatest contribution to the group was: _____

CHECKLIST FOR RATING GROUP MEMBERS

After the importance of group solidarity has become an accepted tenet of the thinking of the majority, it is often beneficial to have students rate all members. The following form has been used for that purpose. It is more appropriate for groups keeping the same personnel for several meetings.

Number the names of members alphabetically.

1. Adams, Ruth   4.   Jones, Ann Marie
2. Bell, Richard   5.   Lee, Edward
3. Harris, John   6.   Swenson, Sandra

Use the corresponding number for the checklist. Rate from 1 (excellent) to 5 (poor).

	Group Members					
	1	2	3	4	5	6
1. Carries out responsibilities	5					
2. Cooperates in discussion	1					
3. Expresses self clearly	1					
4. Considers all viewpoints	2					
5. Encourages others	2					
6. Shows interest in the group's success	5					

Focusing on the evaluation of process can, of course, be overdone. It is useful, at first, as a teaching device to emphasize standards. When students become more adept at group work, it may only be needed rarely.

Figure 4.3

Five Types of

Rating Checklist

(Source Unknown)

in education today is the type of collaborative strategy known as cooperative learning. *Cooperative learning* is the organization of students into teams (small groups) to work toward a common objective by using team rewards, individual accountability, and the opportunity for all to succeed at the task at hand. For example, a teacher would organize the class into small groups (teams of four to five students), give them material to study (e.g., calculating ratios and proportions), assess student learning through quizzes or a game format, and give teams some form of recognition or reward when all members learn the material (Slavin 1980, 1981, 1984).

Cooperative learning activities provide excellent opportunities for discussion, research and sharing, group decision-making, and individual oral presentation skills, and, as such, should have a high priority in a teacher's repertoire of strategies to facilitate student interaction and develop speaking skills.

Why use cooperative learning strategies? Realizing that classes in middle and high school tend to isolate students from friends and peer group, educators developed cooperative learning activities to help build a more caring and supportive learning environment. Research on cooperative learning underscores the value of students speaking and interacting with each other, particularly when compared with more passive, traditional classrooms. Interactive classrooms

help students develop higher level thinking abilities (Hilke 1990). Slavin (1984) found that cooperative learning increases student motivation, leadership skills, self-esteem and feelings of individual responsibility for learning, respect for classmates (including mainstreamed peers and those of other racial and ethnic groups), and time on task. Positive peer relationships (i.e., new friends) develop when students function together as a cohesive group. Those who are "different" often are perceived more favorably (Johnson et al. 1984). These positive peer relationships promote student self-esteem through classroom support groups. By interacting with others in small groups, students learn different strategies and approaches to critical thinking and problem solving (Lyman and Foyle 1990). Finally, classrooms that use cooperative learning strategies stress active communication among students and afford frequent opportunities for students to practice and improve their speaking and communication skills.

Seven Popular Cooperative Learning Strategies

What follows is a brief description of seven popular cooperative learning strategies; five emphasize peer tutoring and two emphasize group investigation. After reviewing them, consider how you might use each strategy, either in a daily lesson plan (e.g., fractions or long division) or with a unit of study in your disci-

pline (e.g., "The Circulatory System" in biology or "The Great Depression and the New Deal" in social studies). Share your thoughts with an educator. What new ideas did you obtain from your partner? (Did you notice we were using a Think/Pair/Share collaborative learning strategy here?)

1. **Teams-Games-Tournament (TGT):**
   - Students are assigned to learning teams of four to five members.
   - Team members study together, trying to make certain every member knows material on worksheets.
   - At week's end, teams compete with one another in simple learning games to develop team score.
   - Scores, and hence, rewards are based on performances of all members of each team.

2. **Student Teams Achievement Divisions (STAD):**
   - Uses same structure as TGT, but uses quizzes instead of games.
   - Takes less time for each lesson and is easier to use.

3. **Round Robin:**
   - Students are grouped in teams of five to six. Each student, in turn, shares something with teammates.
   - This strategy is especially good for review of study questions or unit review.

4. **Numbered Heads Together:**
   - Teacher asks a question.

- In groups of five to six, students consult with each other to see that everyone has the same (correct) answer.
- One student is called upon to respond.

5. **Inside-Outside Circle:**
- Students stand in two concentric circles: inside circle faces out; outside circle faces in.
- When given a review question, each student responds to the student he or she faces; this allows students to check each other's comprehension. They rotate to new partner with each new question.

6. **Jigsaw:**
- Organize class into teams of five to six students.
- Organize content to be studied (unit or part of a unit) into five to six segments.
- Each member of a team is assigned one aspect of the team's topic and becomes an "expert."
- "Experts" from each team meet to discuss their topic and further build expertise.
- "Experts" return to original group and teach members their special topic.
- Students are assessed on all aspects of topic.

7. **Group Investigator:**
- Topic of study (unit or other topic) is divided into subtopics (usually five to six).
- Each subtopic is assigned to a team (five to six members).
- Teams divide topics into individual tasks (one for each member).
- Individuals do investigation and report back to group.
- Group combines individual findings into a group report (written, oral, or both) that is presented to class.
- Students are assessed on all aspects of topic.

Much responsibility falls to the teacher to provide opportunities to engage students in activities where they construct knowledge for themselves—activities that engage students mentally and physically, in this case through the process of interacting with others. To do this teachers need to plan deliberately for student interaction by *facilitating learning*. As we have discussed, two of the most effective ways to do this are through the use of well-focused, whole-class discussions and collaborative small groups. Additionally, individual presentation skills, such as interacting with peers and presenting before the class, are central to students' ability to discuss and work collaboratively with their classmates.

Individual Speaking Opportunities

Interactive secondary school classrooms present many opportunities for students to learn, practice, and extend content while they also hone their speaking skills. Why do teachers assign oral tasks such as research presentations and book reports? Using Figure 4.4, list three benefits that accrue to the teacher, the speaker, and other students.

Benefits		
Teacher	Speaker	Other Students
1. _____	_____	_____
2. _____	_____	_____
3. _____	_____	_____

Figure 4.4
Benefits of
Oral Tasks

The next few pages examine strategies teachers frequently use to underscore the importance of speaking as a learning tool, to showcase student talent, and to build and extend oral communication skills.

Oral Presentations/ Reports

The use of oral presentations and reports is one of the most popular ways of allowing students to solidify their knowledge and share it with others. Frequently, teachers assume students already know how to prepare and deliver oral presentations and reports in an effective manner. Don't make this assumption. Be certain all appropriate techniques are taught to students in advance. Failure to prepare students properly may result in poor learning situations and frustration for both students and teacher. Consider working with another teacher to do the initial instruction. For example, work with your classes' English or social studies teacher. Or, consider working with colleagues to develop grade-level guidelines for oral presentations (see sample guidelines that follow). In this way, all teachers have similar expectations, students benefit from the consistency among teachers, and there is less confusion and increased learning.

Garner (1967) suggests the following five-point approach to preparing an oral presentation or report.

1. Selecting a Subject: Teachers are frequently bound by curricular objectives, and these objectives dictate topics upon which students may be asked to report. Depending upon student age (e.g., sixth vs. eleventh grade) and ability levels, teachers may need to give guidance in how to approach the topic. Specific guide questions may be developed to ensure linkage with teacher objectives and to help students focus their investigation efforts. At other times teachers may wish to open up topic selection to the class. If, for example, a music teacher wanted students to study famous composers (Mozart, Beethoven, Brahms, Schubert, Chopin, etc.) he or she might provide the following guide questions for the small group investigating Beethoven.

- During what era did Beethoven live and what was the cultural environment like in which he created music?
- In what areas were his most significant contributions as a musician and composer?
- List and describe at least five of his most famous works.
- How was Beethoven

viewed by his contemporaries?
- What lasting contributions did Beethoven make to the field of music, as seen by contemporary music historians?
- After reviewing several of Beethoven's works, select your favorite and explain to the class reasons for your selection. Be prepared to play a brief excerpt to the class.

Or, prior to starting a unit on the American Civil War, a social studies teacher might conduct a brainstorming session asking students what they already know about the Civil War and what specifically they would like to learn about as they begin their study. In a matter of minutes, the chalkboard could be filled with a multitude of student ideas suitable for investigation and oral presentations.

2. Organizing the Oral Presentation/Report: Teach students the following structure for an oral presentation.

- Introduction: Have some way to get the audience's attention (i.e., a "motivation!"). If you regularly motivate your students, they can use your teaching as a model. Notice our use of purpose-for-reading activities at the beginning of each chapter of this text. Students can easily adapt this approach by cuing classmates to listening and viewing as they make their presentations. Students should state the

central idea or purpose of the presentation/ report. Both the speaker and the audience need purpose and direction. "If you don't know where you are going, you are liable to end up somewhere else!" (Mager 1984). Often, a good question to provoke audience thinking or a situation/story that catches audience attention works well. For example, a student in French class giving a report on the culture of Brittany might begin by asking the other students if they have ever tasted crepes, and, if so, what their composition is, and how they liked them.
- Body: Includes main ideas and supporting facts and arguments to develop the central purpose of the report.
- Summary/Conclusion: Contains a cogent summary or set of statements regarding conclusions and/or recommendations.

3. Supporting Main Idea/ Purpose: Encourage students to cite authorities where appropriate; describe cause and effect relationships; use supporting statistics; give examples and illustrations; and employ visual aids. These approaches enhance students' abilities in terms of speaking to learn, both as speaker and listener. In addition to the obvious use of visuals, such as charts, diagrams, and pictures, suggest that students "dress the part." For example, a math student might come to class dressed as Pythagorus, the mathematician who contributed to the development of mnemonics as well as geometric theorems. While presenting, the student might dialogue with the class as if it were ancient times.

4. Preparing the Oral Presentation: Have students first develop a topic outline or web (see Chapters 3 and 5) of their presentation and then expand that into a sentence outline. Developing a written report to accompany their presentation may also be a good idea. This is especially helpful for novice oral presenters; it helps them develop their thoughts in a logical and complete manner, making summary notes an easy task later. Many teachers believe that oral presentations are improved by the submission of written reports at the time of the oral presentation. The writing process lays the groundwork for the speaking process. Finally, students need to place their key ideas on note cards 3×5, 4×6, or 5×8, whichever size seems most comfortable. Suggestions for note card organization include that they be: limited in number (two to six), front-side only, and employ a brief topic outline. Once developed, students should rehearse their presentation. Effective presentations require that students know their topic and practice their delivery.

5. Delivery: Noyes and Dickson (1969) offer some helpful guidelines for presenters in the form of questions to

ask themselves.

- Can I be heard?
- Can I be understood (clear articulation, voice expression, and tone)?
- Am I concise and to the point?
- Am I interesting? If not, what can I do to make myself so (expressive voice, enthusiasm, humor, illustrations)?
- Do I look self-confident and poised?
- What type of physical movements can make my presentation more effective (posture, gestures, body movement, eye movement, and facial expressions)?
- Am I smiling? (Smiling relaxes the audience as well as oneself.)

After oral presentations, teachers should give students helpful feedback based on previously established guidelines. There should be no surprises here! Some criteria to consider are: content coverage, use of notes, voice projection, poise, proper use of language, voice tone and inflection, verbal emphasis, transitions, focus on and summarizing around key ideas, and the use of visual aids. When appropriate, the teacher can distribute a simple checklist to solicit feedback from the class that can also serve to reinforce the importance of good speaking skills. See Figure 4.5 for a sample checklist a teacher might use to give students feedback on their oral research presentation. Be sensitive to the fact that students can become too critical of one an-

other's efforts. Work to avoid situations that contribute to increased anxiety levels.

Teachers need to be certain to foster supportive environments for student presentations. It should be "OK" not to present as well as others. "Stage fright" needs to be diffused as much as possible. Teachers should give some thought to where they position themselves when students are speaking. Some students feel more secure if the teacher stands near them; others are more at ease if the teacher is in the front or back of the classroom. Some students will need the use of a lectern. Teachers also need to give special consideration to any in-class reaction or evaluation they render after the completion of student presentations. All students need immediate praise on some aspect of their performance; this helps to diffuse fear in speaking situations, which could impact negatively on a student's ability to "speak and learn" in the future. Always be sensitive to student self-esteem, especially when adolescents perform in front of their peers. The aim should be to help individual students grow (extend their knowledge and performance skills), not to identify and reward the best speakers in the class. A popular strategy used by teachers to give feedback to students is the PQP strategy (Praise/Question/Polish), where teachers react in terms of praiseworthy elements, ask a question or two about aspects of the presentation (content, delivery, etc.) and make one or

Name _____

CONTENT	EVALUATION	COMMENTS
Did the speaker:		
1. arouse interest with the introduction?		
2. present ideas in a clearly organized manner?		
3. share ideas that were crucial to the thesis?		
4. include at least one quotation from a source used in the project?		
5. keep major points to a few in number?		
6. summarize the project clearly?		
ORAL STYLE		
7. observe the time limit?		
8. use language appropriate to the purpose and the audience?		
9. use notes only as a reference?		
10. use standard English?		
11. unify the message through the arrangement of information and ideas?		

Superior........5 points   A = 60–49 points   **TOTAL**
Very Good.....4 points   **POINTS** _____
Good.............3 points   B = 48-37 points
Fair................2 points
Poor..............1 point   C= 36-25 points   **GRADE** _____
(Baltimore County Board of Education: English Office, no date)

Figure 4.5

Checklist for

Oral Presentation

two helpful suggestions. It is a simple yet effective strategy.

Role Playing and Creative Dramatics
When is the last time you experienced a teacher, particularly at the college or university level, use role playing or creative drama in the classroom? Probably not too frequently! Here are some role-playing possibilities from secondary school classrooms.

- In drama class, have students role-play two theater/drama critics, such as Siskal and Ebert, as they critique current movies or theatrical productions.
- A middle school science teacher might orchestrate the "CO2 Ballet," in which some students become trees that give off other students, representing oxygen. The oxygen travels into another group of students who represent human beings, at which time they join with other students who represent carbon. The carbon pops out of the humans and floats across the classroom to be sucked in by the trees—from which oxygen emerges.
- The instrumental music teacher might have several students, each at different times, role-play a conductor who is directing a score with an orchestra.
- In Spanish class, one student could role-play a waiter and several others patrons as they order dinner in an expensive restaurant in Madrid.
- In social studies, students might role-play Abraham Lincoln and his cabinet deciding whether to reinforce Fort Sumter, which precipitated the start of the Civil War.

What value is there in this approach for students? Is there

any value for the teacher? Using Figure 4.6, list three experiences you have had with role playing or dramatics in the classroom (middle, high, or college), and describe the value of the experience from a student's and teacher's point of view. Then, compare your chart with the benefits described in the following paragraph.

Role playing actively engages students in the learning process (physically and mentally); increases their motivational level; and builds thinking, listening, and speaking skills (Good and Brophy 1991). It helps students deal with academic content in real and personalized ways. In role playing, students act out the behavior of a person, other than themselves, as they see that individual behaving in real life. Most often it is spontaneous and unrehearsed. Properly implemented, role playing permits the teacher to engage the entire class intellectually, verbally, and physically, as it explores a problem in science class, literature, social studies, health, foreign language, even art class. For example, in social studies, students might role-play Columbus and his crew as they wrestle with his decision to abort their search for the New World. Or, health students might role-play a scenario in which one of them is attempting to resist the peer pressure of the rest of the group, all of whom want to use an illegal drug. In English class, students may create a monologue for Tom Sawyer who is trying to convince his friends of the joys of white-washing his Aunt Polly's fence. Many pieces of literature present wonderful opportunities for students to express their views and values by role-playing alternative scenarios (e.g., *Hamlet* and *Julius Caesar* (Shakespeare), *Red Badge of Courage* (Crane), *The Chocolate War* (Cormier), *A Separate Peace* (Knowles), and *Jacob Have I Loved* (Paterson). Role-playing situations are easy for teachers to design. (For more information on role playing, see Shaftel and Shaftel 1967).

Role playing is an excellent way to engage students in cognitive interactions and interpersonal exchanges. For example, students can engage in lively debate over whether history should regard President Truman as a hero or a war criminal. Or, students could role-play alternative scenarios to Jerry's actions in the *Chocolate War*, exploring whether or not he was a flawed hero. Role playing employs a verbal model (rather than a physical or mathematical one) that requires thoughtful speech and focused student interactions, which in turn facilitates reflective and critical thinking, develops group cohesiveness, and improves self-concepts (Shaftel and Shaftel 1967). In their book, *Role Playing for Social Values*, Shaftel and Shaftel (1967) explore the follow-ing helpful steps to organizing role playing activities in the classroom.

1. "Warming up" the group (identifying and discussing the problem under consideration)
2. Selecting the participants (role players)
3. Preparing the audience to participate as observers
4. Setting the stage (brief preparation by role players)
5. Role-playing (actual enactment)
6. Discussing and evaluating
7. Further enactments (replaying revised roles, suggested next steps or possible alternatives)
8. Further discussion (debriefing)
9. Sharing experiences and generalizing

Plays and dramatic productions such as role playing, afford opportunities for students to depict characters other than themselves and provide a wonderful outlet for student (and teacher) creativity. The dramatic "production"

Role Playing/Drama in the Classroom

Experiences	Value to Students	Value to Teacher
1. _____		
2. _____		
3. _____		

Figure 4.6
Values of
Role Playing

may be spontaneous and unrehearsed (such as role playings or improvisations), or it may be a structured, practiced activity (a play) in which students know exactly what each player will say and do. Each of these approaches requires students to speak, often in very dramatic ways, and to interact with others while learning about the subject under study (Chapin and Gross 1973). Students can research and write scripts or work from existing manuscripts. For example, in health class, students might create a skit about homeless people in their city, with a special focus on nutrition, communicable diseases, and health-care problems. In English class, students might create a play about life in a New York City's immigrant ghetto in the late nineteenth century by using Thornton Wilder's play *Our Town* as a model; or in social studies, they might write a play about the Boston Massacre as contemporary research suggests it happened.

Panels and Debates

A good method for emphasizing students' oral language and public speaking skills is to incorporate panels and formal debates into the curriculum (Woolever and Scott 1988). Both require advance preparation on the part of students in the form of reading, research, and organization. Knowing they have to use information in an improvisational way may motivate students to do the research and to prepare for the experience of responding ex-

temporaneously before the class. The use of improvisation helps students clarify and reorganize their knowledge base—in short, to construct knowledge for themselves and to help others do the same. Panels have widespread application where teachers wish selected students to present different views on a topic (e.g., the "greenhouse effect" and its implications) while the remainder of the class (after appropriate background reading) engage panelists in a dialogue about the topic. Panel "experts" provide depth and opinion on the topic, while the audience's knowledge is extended.

Debates are more limited in their applicability, in that they employ formal rules and procedures that require student training to execute with proficiency. They present excellent opportunities, however, for selected students to engage in in-depth research on a topic and to spar with other students in intellectual discourse, sharpening their research, thinking, and verbal skills. Formal debates can also be excellent experiences for the listening, nonparticipating audience. As with any valuable experience, teachers need to design ways to mentally involve the audience and "debrief" the debate in terms of lesson objectives. For example, in a panel where four major ideas or views are presented, the teacher might organize the audience into four groups, each responsible for later summarizing presenter's key ideas and for raising questions de-

signed to clarify, probe, or seek additional information. In a debate setting, observers might be asked to rate the breadth, depth, and power of each speaker's argument (listing specific points for each), and to evaluate the debate as a whole.

Interviews

Having students interview or be interviewed is a valuable strategy in developing students' oral language skills (Phelan 1989). In-class interviews give the teacher the opportunity to provide students with feedback on their speaking ability. They also provide, for the students, a creative way of processing academic content and information. For example, one student might interview another who poses as a noted critic of the works of John Steinbeck; or after researching Einstein's theory of relativity, a student explains it to the class as he is interviewed by a student news reporter for the school paper. In physical education class, students might interview a local sports hero; while in a modern language class, they could interview an exchange student regarding life and culture in his or her homeland.

Using oral history techniques (Martorella 1991) permits students to learn first-hand from the experience of those who have witnessed history. These interviews can be shared with peers through audiotapes, videotapes, or in-class presentations and are excellent ways of increasing student motivation and building student confidence and social interaction skills. Developing student skills as oral historians requires monitoring and supervision by the teacher, particularly in the preparation of student-interview questions and the selection and scheduling of interviewees. When interacting with the community, remind students that the reputation of the school and the teacher come into play.

Book Talks

Having students share information about books they are reading (required reading or free choice) is a good way to get even the most timid student talking, especially if the setting is a small, nonthreatening group (Phelan 1989) and one that is stimulating to all involved. When book talks are brief and follow a focused format (such as key questions), they can be stimulating to both speaker and audience, especially if those listening have an opportunity to interact with the speaker afterward. Small groups of four to five students are good settings for book talks, but there are other creative (and often more stimulating) ways to share stimulating ideas found in books.

- After reading an historical account, students could incorporate important information into a news article and either deliver it in TV news-show fashion, or develop, along with other students, a newspaper front page for distribution to the class or for display on a bulletin board.

- Math students who read biographies/autobiographies of major mathematicians could use visual/mathematical illustrations representing their person as the cornerstone of their presentation; in this way, presentations would be highly visual and focus clearly on the contributions of the mathematician.

- Science students who read a book on an assigned topic (e.g., nuclear energy, star physics, or black holes) could develop book talks for an audience of younger children (perhaps third grade), requiring them to simplify the major concepts and maybe even to use visual aids.

Tips for Teachers in Fostering Speaking Skills

Here are some special caveats for teachers who use speaking activities with students.

1. Wait Time: If you want to increase students' solicited and unsolicited verbal responses in class, student questions, student-to-student interactions, and inference drawing, simply provide more wait time between the question and calling on a student to respond. Rowe (1974) in a remarkable study found that teachers:

. . . waited less than one second before calling on someone to respond. Furthermore, even after calling on a student, they waited only about a second for a student to give the answer before supplying it themselves.

Give students time to think, and do not do their thinking for them. Good speakers are also good listeners. Quiet time facilitates student reflection, and reflection fosters thinking, all of which is manifested in student verbal dialogue in class.

2. Group Size: Give careful thought to the selection of groups. Too many students in a group (whether discussion or work group) impede its effectiveness. The ideal small discussion group is from four to six students. Collaborative and cooperative learning groups vary in size, from as low as two students to as high as six. Critical to the size of the group is the complexity of the task at hand and specificity of the directions given.

3. Tape Discussions: Consider taping (audio or video) student discussions. It permits students to analyze their performance, that of others, and the group as a whole. Tapes can be debriefed as a class or individually, permitting the teacher to focus on particular skill development.

4. Student Sensitivity: Be sensitive to:

- shy and withdrawn students
- student self-esteem
- students who speak English as their second language
- Students from families and communities where standard English is not spoken

- Students whose speaking skills are not as developed as those of other students.

SUMMARY

The learning strategies described in this chapter—entire class discussion, collaborative small groups, cooperative learning, oral presentations/reports, role playings, creative dramatics, panels and debates, interviews, and book talks—all serve to actively engage students cognitively and physically, and at times even emotionally, causing them to interact with classmates and the teacher on a range of intellectual levels. As students put thought into speech and refine their thinking through verbal interaction with others, their learning of content is reinforced, thinking skills are sharpened, language-processing skills are practiced, and social skills and self-esteem are enhanced.

Finally, speaking more effectively is an important language skill necessary for success in school and in life. Speaking provides students opportunities, through interactions with teacher and peers, to construct knowledge for themselves, connecting prior learning to present input and facilitating the movement of knowledge from short-term memory into long-term memory. As with any skill, students acquire it when given sustained practice to imbed the skill in their repertoire of behaviors. Speaking demands students be active learners, requiring them to process content and learning experiences as they interact with others in an interactive environment—the classroom. It is important, therefore, that teachers design a variety of speaking experiences into class activities if students are to be active learners and effective speakers.

BIBLIOGRAPHY

- Chapin, J.R., and Gross, R.E. *Teaching Social Studies Skills.* Boston: Little, Brown, 1973.

- Dickens, M. *Speech: Dynamic Communication.* San Diego, Calif.: Harcourt, Brace, Jovanovich, 1973.

- Fausti, R.P., and McGlone, E.L. *Understanding Oral Communication.* Menlo Park, Calif.: Cummings, 1972.

- Garner, D.L. *Idea to Delivery: A Handbook of Oral Communication.* Belmont, Calif.: Dickenson, 1967.

- Good, T.L., and Brophy, J.E. *Looking in Classrooms.* Fifth edition. New York: Harper Collins, 1991.

- Goodlad, J. *A Place Called School.* New York: McGraw-Hill, 1984.

- Grambs, J.D., and Carr, J.C. *Modern Methods in Secondary Education.* Fifth edition. Fort Worth, Tex.: Holt, Rinehart, and Winston, 1991.

- Gronbeck, B.E. *The Articulate Person.* Glenview, Ill.: Scott Foresman, 1979.

- Hilke, V.E. *Cooperative Learning.* Bloomington, Ind.: Phi Delta Kappa, 1990.

- Jackson, R.H. "Advocacy Before the Supreme Court: Suggestions for Effective Case Presentations." *American Bar Association Journal* 37 (1951): 803, as cited in *Speech: Dynamic Communication*, by Dickens, M. San Diego, Calif.: Harcourt, Brace, Jovanovich, 1974.

- Johnson, D.W., Johnson, R.T., Holubec, E.J., and Roy, P. *Circle of Learning: Cooperation in the Classroom.* Alexandria, Va.: Association for Supervision and Curriculum Development, 1984.

- Lyman L., and Foyle, H.C. *Cooperative Grouping for Interactive Learning.* Washington, D.C.: National Education Association, 1990.

- Mager, R. *Preparing Instructional Objectives.* Revised second edition. Belmont, Calif.: David S. Lake, 1984.

- Mahood, W., Biemer, L., and Lowe, W.T. *Teaching Social Studies in Middle and High Schools.* New York: Merrill, 1991.

- Martorella, P.H. *Teaching Social Studies in Middle and Secondary Schools.* New York: Macmillan, 1991.

- Milner, J.O., and Milner, L.F. *Bridging English.* Merrill: New York, 1993.

- Moffett, J., and Wagner, B.J. *Student-Centered Language Arts, K–12.* Fourth edition. Portsmouth, N.H.: Boynton-Cook and Heinemann, 1992, as cited in *Bridging English*, by Milner, J. and Milner, L.F. Merrill: New York, 1993.

- Myers, C.B., and Myers, L.K. *An Introduction to Teaching and Schools*. Fort Worth, Tex.: Holt, Rinehart, and Winston, 1990.

- Neubert, G.A., and Binko, J.B. *Inductive Reasoning in the Secondary Classroom*. Washington, D.C.: National Education Association, 1992.

- Noyes, W., and Dickson, C.W. *Core Knowledge for Successful Speech*. Atlanta, Ga.: Scott Foresman, 1969.

- Phelan, P. *Classroom Practices in Teaching English*, vol. 24. Urbana, Ill.: National Council of Teachers of English, 1989.

- Rowe, M.B. "Wait Time and Rewards as Instructional Variables," *Journal of Research in Science Teaching* 11 (1974): 81–94.

- Shaftel, F.R., and Shaftel, G. *Role Playing for Social Values*. Englewood Cliffs, N.J.: Prentice-Hall, 1967.

- Shepherd, D.L. *Comprehensive High School Reading Methods*. Columbus, Ohio: Charles Merrill, 1972.

- Slavin, R.E. "Effects of Student Teams and Peer Tutoring on Academic Achievement and Time on Task." *Journal of Experimental Education* 48 (1980): 252–57.

- ____. "Student Team Learning." *Elementary School Journal* 82 (1981): 5–17.

- ____. "Students Motivating Students to Excel: Cooperative Incentives, Cooperative Tasks, and Student Achievement." *Elementary School Journal* 85 (1984): 53–63.

- Staton, J. *Thinking Together: Language Interaction in Children's Reasoning*. Washington, D.C.: Dingle Associates, 1983.

- Tonjes, M.J., and Zintz, M.V. *Teaching Reading, Thinking, and Study Skills in Content Classrooms*. Third edition. Dubuque, Iowa: William C. Brown, 1992.

- Woolever R., and Scott, K.P. *Active Learning in Social Studies*. Glenview, Ill.: Scott Foresman, 1988

Practice

1. Recall your days in middle and high school. Can you remember any experiences giving oral reports and presentations, either individually or in groups? What are your recollections? In general, were these positive learning experiences? Why? Why not? Did you like giving reports and making presentations? What type of guidelines did your teachers have? Can you think of ways they might have improved upon the experience?

2. Select a unit topic in your subject area (e.g., "Lyric Poetry," "The American Civil War and Reconstruction," or "Interaction of Matter and Energy") and develop a series of topics within the unit suitable for individual or small group oral presentations and research reports. This could be either at the middle school or high school level. Develop a set of guidelines to give students, detailing your expectations for oral presentations. Be specific.

3. Think of your professional education courses. Did any of the instructors use collaborative small groups? Rate the quality of the collaborative small groups in which you participated in these courses (high to low, with five representing high). What made these experiences valuable or ineffective? What suggestions could you make to improve your instructors' use of collaborative small groups? Rate your instructors' use of entire class discussions in the same manner.

4. Imagine yourself as a first year teacher. As you begin to organize for the year, what expectations will you have of your students when they speak and respond in class? How can these expectations help students acquire new knowledge, sharpen thinking skills, get important practice in language processing, increase their social interaction skills, and build self-esteem?

5. If you were to work with another teacher who teaches the same sections as you, but on a different grade level (e.g., English, science, social studies, etc.), how could you work cooperatively to enhance students' learning through speaking activities?

6. Interview several teachers in your subject area. Ask them the following questions to determine their feelings about use of student oral presentation/report skills.

   • Do you assess students speaking and oral presentation skills early in the school year and before assigning these experiences to students?

   • Can you describe a unit you teach that incorporates oral reporting and presentation skills? If not, why not? If so, how do you incorporate these skills into the unit?

   • Do you prefer individual oral reports over group reports? Why? Why not? Do you value both? If so, when is one more appropriate than the other?

   • Are students given specific guidelines for presentation of their reports? If so, what are those guidelines?

   • Do you give students feedback, either orally or in writing, on their oral presentation? If so, please elaborate.

7. How could you provide special assistance to students in your classes who are very timid about speaking in front of their peers? How might you work to diffuse their fears and still help them make progress in speaking before others so that they continually accrue learning benefits associated with verbal interaction and oral proficiency?

8. Create at least one small group activity that Ms. Jones of Chapter 1 could incorporate into her lesson that would cause students to speak to learn.

CLASSROOM CARRY-OVER

Here's how I plan to use what I just learned about speaking in the interactive classroom.

_____

_____

_____

_____

_____

_____

_____

_____

_____

_____

_____

_____

_____

_____

_____

_____

_____

_____

_____

_____

_____

_____

_____

_____

_____

_____

_____

_____

CHAPTER 5

Reading in the Interactive Classroom

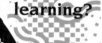

How do you use reading activities to encourage learning?

READINESS

Upon initial consideration, it seems as if the process of reading is, by its very nature, a solitary act. And yet reading is an activity that requires an active stance on the part of the reader if comprehension—real reading—is to take place. How do you, as a reader, keep yourself actively engaged and, therefore, comprehending during reading?

Reading aids learning; therefore, reading is used widely in the secondary content areas as a learning tool. From your experience, how do secondary teachers use interaction in the classroom to facilitate student understanding of what they read?

Purpose for Reading

The reading material in this chapter should help you answer the following questions.

1. What is "reading?"
2. What are the implications of theory and research for the teaching of reading vocabulary and the facilitation of comprehension in the content areas?
3. What interactive strategies can be used in the classroom to facilitate better comprehension of content-reading material?

READING MATERIAL

This section takes a comprehensive look at the reading process and its relationship to learning.

The Reading Process

Read the paragraph below and answer the three questions (Gutkoska) that follow it.

State Champions

John Martin knew that the entire contest rested on his shoulders. With the score 19-18 in favor of State High, John realized that his match with Bill Favor would determine the state championship. With the speed and cunning of a fox, Bill Favor from Alton High managed to take down and near fall in the first few seconds of the match. Through two and one-half periods, the score remained the same, but finally in the closing seconds of the final period John managed a reversal. The students from State High were thrilled and screamed with delight. Shortly later, the bell sounded. The contest had come to the end. At last, the championship had been decided.

Questions

1. In what type of activity are the youngsters engaged?
2. What was the final team score?
3. Who was the better "foot person?"

If you had difficulty answering the questions, it is because you probably have not had sufficient background in watching and scoring wrestling. If you could answer the questions, you obviously have spent some time observing or participating in wrestling.

Reading is a process whereby the reader interacts with the text in order to construct meaning. It is a process of relating what we already know to the information in the reading, that is, matching our background of experience, our cognitive structure, to what the author of the reading is saying. Without sufficient background, we cannot comprehend.

Reading is used primarily in the secondary classroom as a learning tool. Learning is a process of modifying and elaborating our cognitive structure.

Successful comprehension occurs when the reader has sufficient background to connect the new information to the old. It is the content teacher's responsibility to facilitate learning in the secondary classroom by considering the background students need in order to comprehend assigned reading material. This facilitation involves: (1) developing students' background in content as well as in vocabulary and (2) using interactive lesson approaches that will maximize student comprehension and learning.

Content Vocabulary

It is through vocabulary, the understanding of the meaning of individual words, that the concepts and principles of the content area are communicated. A positive correlation exists between vocabulary and comprehension. In other words, the more vocabulary the reader understands, the more comprehension of the reading passage should occur.

The secondary content teacher should not assume that students will learn the vocabulary of the content incidentally, that is, as a by-product of lessons or reading. New content vocabulary, which is essential to comprehend the upcoming reading, must be taught directly and prior to students' first encounter with the reading .

How did your teachers help you to learn content vocabulary? Do you recall your teachers presenting words prior to reading? Other than having you look words up in the dictionary, what other strategies did they use to help you learn content vocabulary?

Experience and research has shown that vocabulary "priming" , that is, teaching pertinent vocabulary words prior to reading, is best accomplished by presenting new and difficult vocabulary in a way that requires the learner to become actively engaged in determining the meaning of the words (Nelson-Herber 1986), as opposed to locating definitions in a dictionary or glossary or being given the meanings by the teacher. The latter two approaches are passive approaches in which students are the recipients of the authors' or the teachers' processed knowledge. The dictionary approach carries with it an additional complication for learning content vocabulary because dictionary definitions often contain other words that are unfamiliar to the students. For example, if sent to a glossary to learn the meaning of *plateau*, students might encounter the following definition: a tableland. This definition probably does little to clarify the concept of *plateau*. But, if the social studies teacher shows the students pictures of plateaus, students should have no difficulty understanding and generating a definition in their own words that can be recorded and referred to for future use.

There are many interactive strategies that the content teacher can use for vocabulary priming. Four will be described here. They are: (1) concrete representations, (2) context clues, (3) imaging, and (4) concept attainment.

1. Concrete Representations: Concrete representations facilitate the learning of word meanings ("a picture is worth a thousand words"), and many content vocabulary words do lend themselves to such direct associations. Pictures, models, and actual demonstrations also add a novelty effect to the lesson that helps in maintaining the attention of the students (a requirement for learning). For example, an English teacher who will have students read *Rikki-Tikki-Tavi* will need to prime the word, *mongoose*, if he or she believes the concept is not part of students' background, because the mongoose is one of the central characters. The most efficient way to teach this word is to show a picture of a mongoose and after directing students' attention to particular aspects of the picture, have the students generate a definition/ description of a mongoose. In a similar way, a health teacher could teach the word, *esophagus* by using a model of the human head and throat. The home economics teacher could teach cotton vs. wool by having students examine actual samples of the fibers. The science teacher could teach several vocabulary words by having students examine a magnetic compass. The social studies teacher could help students define *descendent* by using the term as he or she shows pictures of a famous person and that person's parents and children. The music teacher could demonstrate *staccato* by playing several bars of music in this fashion. The physical education teacher could perform a *lob* for the students.

2. Context Clues: Not all content vocabulary, however, lends itself readily, or at all, to concrete representation. For example, the geography teacher might teach *erosion* by presenting this statement and having students who live on the east coast use their background of experience to define/explain the process of erosion.

The Atlantic beaches are currently being re-shaped by bulldozers in order to get them ready for the summer tourist season. This is necessary because of the *erosion* the beaches suffered during the winter storms.

The English teacher who wishes to teach students the general vocabulary word, *affluent* could present the following sentence as the clue from which the students can generate a definition.

My Aunt Teresa is quite *affluent*. She has a winter and summer home, an apartment in New York, a private jet, and wears only Chanel suits.

Although students do not know this "aunt," they can generate a definition based on the clues provided in the sentences.

To test the utility of context-clue usage, try to determine the meaning of the underlined word in the following sentence.

Dad added *ufrasis* to the taco meat to give it a hearty flavor.

Actually, *ufrasis* is a nonsense word, that is, a word we made up, but chances are you could still determine our intention that *ufrasis* is a spice or flavoring, thus proving the power of context clues for learning new vocabulary.

3. Imaging: Another strategy for teaching vocabulary is imaging, or visualization, a process of creating a picture in the mind. This process lends itself well to helping students create a picture when one is not available or when the concept can be represented only by describing incidents that demonstrate the concept. For example, the science teacher who wants students to learn the term, *symbiosis* (or *mutualism*), might have students close their eyes and visualize the following oral description.

You are standing on a grassy plain in Africa. It is very warm. The tall grass reaches over your boots, up to your knees. At a safe distance in front of you, is a female rhinoceros. She is quite large. Gnats and flies circle her body, and she tries to use her tail to swat them from her head. You watch for a few minutes. (Pause.) Now, a small bird flies near, and comes to rest on the neck of the rhinoceros. Some of the gnats and flies are scared off by this new arrival. The bird begins to eat the remaining gnats and flies. Watch the bird eat. (Pause.) This relationship between the rhino and bird is an example of *symbiosis*. Open your eyes now, and write a draft of your definition of *symbiosis*.

A social studies teacher might find imaging a successful strategy for teaching *barter*; the English teacher for teaching *gullible*; a mathematics teacher for *assets*; a music teacher for *mood*. What vocabulary words from your content area might be well-suited for imaging?

4. Concept Attainment: Concept attainment is a type of inductive strategy. Induction requires the learner to examine specifics and formulate a generalization that applies to all the specific examples. During concept attainment, the teacher presents examples and nonexamples of the concept and asks students to write a definition after examining the samples. Figure 5.1 shows how a math teacher could teach the term, *polygon*. The students would be instructed to examine the two lists and then to list the characteristics of a *polygon*. In doing so, they will have defined a *polygon*.

A similar presentation format could be used by the art teacher to teach *impressionism*, or by the social studies

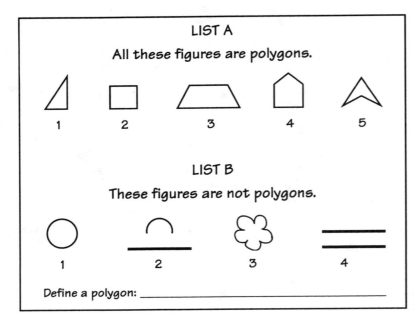

LIST A

All these figures are polygons.

1 2 3 4 5

LIST B

These figures are not polygons.

1 2 3 4

Define a polygon: _____

Figure 5.1

Using Concept Attainment

To Teach Vocabulary

teacher to teach *covert operations*. What vocabulary from your content area could be presented via concept attainment?

Sometimes concept attainment is used to teach two closely related concepts by presenting examples of each simultaneously. For example, the English teacher might present one list of examples labeled *alliteration*, and a second list labeled *assonance* and have the students distinguish the two by identifying distinguishing characteristics. The science teacher might teach *herbivore* and *carnivore* simultaneously; the typing teacher, *invoice* and *memo*; the health teacher, *stimulant* and *depressant*.

5. Vocabulary Priming Process: Notice that the four strategies previously explained—concrete representations, context clues, imaging, concept attainment—encourage an interactive classroom environment. The teacher provides the clues, based on the students' experience, but it is the students who engage in active cognitive processing during their initial exposure to the clues and then articulate the definitions. The students are interacting with the clues in order to construct their own meaning. Neither the teacher nor the dictionary/glossary presents the students with the definitions in final form. The understanding of the new vocabulary expands students' background experience, which in turn, facilitates comprehension of the upcoming reading material. This interactive vocabulary presentation is called the *vocabulary-priming process*.

Content teachers have found that this process also provides opportunities for interaction through student collaboration. It is ideally suited to incorporating the Think-Pair-Share technique (Lyman 1981, McTighe and Lyman 1988). During the initial exposure to the clues through concrete representations, context clues, imaging, concept attainment, or some other active learning strategy, students first *think* about and draft their own definition of the vocabulary word. Then students *pair* with a nearby classmate, discuss their definitions, and revise them as needed. Finally, through an entire class discussion, the pairs *share* their definitions, and a final class definition is reached through revision and consensus. This final definition is recorded in the students content vocabulary notebook for future reference and review.

Comprehension

The first part of this chapter dealt with interactive strategies that facilitate students' learning of content vocabulary words. We now turn our attention to interactive lesson approaches that facilitate students' comprehension of whole text—vocabulary words combined into sentence, sentences combined into paragraphs, and paragraphs combined into complete reading selections.

Reading comprehension is the understanding of material read. When we observe students reading silently, it appears that they are passively absorbing what someone else has written. However, comprehension cannot take place unless students are interacting cognitively with the reading material. It is, therefore, the content teachers' responsibility to plan activities and lessons that facilitate this interaction.

Several interactive reading strategies that encourage cognitive engagement on the part of the student are described here. They are: (1) graphic organizers, (2) Directed Reading Activities, (3) Directed-Reading-Thinking Activities, (4)

Directed Inquiry Activities, (5) the Independent Comprehension Strategy, (6) strategies for word problems in math, and (7) reader response.

Graphic Organizers

A *graphic organizer* is a teaching strategy that provides "written and pictorial structure to a body of content material, thus providing a visual pathway (graphic organizer) to couple with a verbal pathway (reading/lecture/discussion)" (Hawk and McLeod 1983). Graphic organizers include time lines, Venn diagrams, flowcharts, labeled pictures, webs or semantic maps, and comparative feature charts. Formal research and classroom experience have shown that graphic organizers are most effective in increasing the achievement of secondary students (Hawk, McLeod and Jeane 1981, McTighe 1986). They can be used in conjunction with reading as well as with listening, speaking, and writing as a guided note-taking strategy.

Figure 5.2 shows a participatory Venn diagram that eighth graders completed as they read about French and Spanish life in the New World. Inherent in a Venn diagram are the thinking skills of comparison and contrast because information unique to each group is written in the appropriate outside circle, while facts shared by the two groups are written in the overlapping area. Thus the comparison-contrast element is highlighted by the visual component of the diagram.

Another popular type of participatory graphic organizer for reading is the comparative feature chart. Figures 5.3 and 5.4 are two examples. Figure 5.3 is designed for an English class that is reading a series of myths about Greek heroes. Figure 5.4 is designed for a science class that is reading about the chemical elements of the earth.

Because they provide a visual presentation of the facts, each of these comparative feature charts facilitates student recognition of the similarities and differences among the elements. As students read, they complete the charts, and this focused attention and writing facilitates active reading and thus improves comprehension. When students complete the charts, the teacher can help them examine the facts in order to recognize patterns and thus articulate generalizations. For example, by noting similarities among the facts on the Greek classical hero chart (Figure 5.3), students can generalize the essential characteristics of a classical hero. (See Chapter 3 for other examples of graphic organizers to use in conjunction with reading.)

Directed Reading Activity

The Directed Reading Activity (DRA) was originally developed by Emmett Betts (1946) for use in elementary grades. This lesson-plan format has also been quite successful in actively engaging secondary students in all content areas when instructional reading material is to be used to learn the concepts and principles of the discipline.

Directed Reading Activty 5.1 (at end of chapter) is a DRA that was developed for an eighth grade English class involved in a unit on choices writers make. This lesson focuses on decisions authors have characters make. Eventually, these students will write their own narratives in which they will have characters make decisions. As you read the plan, identify: (1) the five steps of the activity and (2) the purpose of each step.

As you read this DRA, you, no doubt, were able to identify the following five steps.

1. **Readiness**
   a. *Motivation*
   b. *Developing and/or Tapping Background of Experience*
   c. *Concept Development*
   d. *Purpose for Reading*
2. **Silent Reading**
3. **Discussion**
4. **Re-Reading**
5. **Follow-Up**

Notice that the first step, Readiness, has four phases—Motivation, Background of Experience, Concept Development, and Purpose for Reading. The overall purpose of the Readiness stage of the DRA is to prepare students to read content material. Without such preparation, the reading would be insufficiently comprehensible to the students.

As with most lessons, the DRA begins with Motivation (1a), an activity designed to focus the students' attention on the topic for the lesson and to capture their interest. Note in the DRA lesson that interest and attention to the topic

Figure 5.2
Venn Diagram

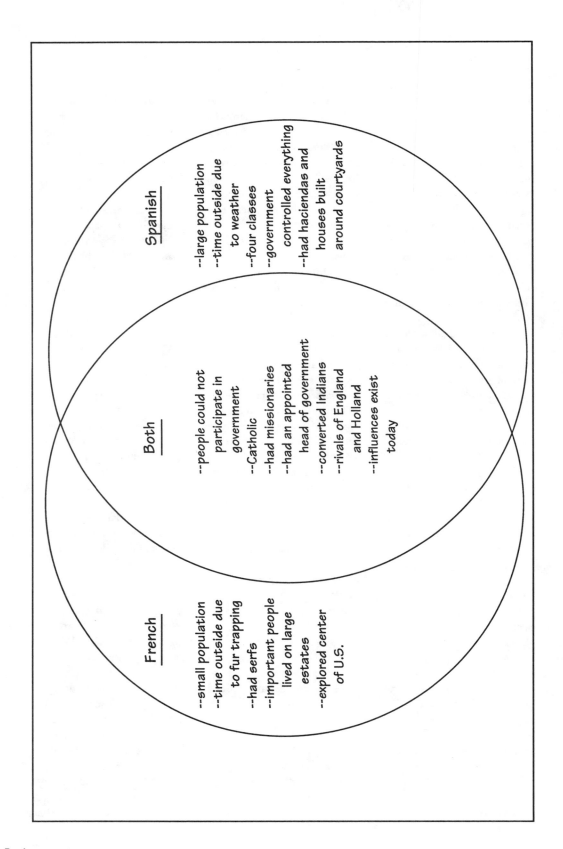

Spanish

--large population
--time outside due
   to weather
--four classes
--government
   controlled everything
--had haciendas and
   houses built
   around courtyards

Both

--people could not
   participate in
   government
--Catholic
--had missionaries
--had an appointed
   head of government
--converted Indians
--rivals of England
   and Holland
--influences exist
   today

French

--small population
--time outside due
   to fur trapping
--had serfs
--important people
   lived on large
   estates
--explored center
   of U.S.

of "decision," was accomplished by having the teacher relate personal decisions and then having students write about an important decision they have made.

The Background of Experience phase (1b) finds the teacher asking the students to recall what they already know about the topic of the lesson and providing students with necessary background if such is lacking. This development of background can be in the form of a mini-lecture, a class discussion, a film, a demonstration, an audio recording, and so on. The primary purpose of this stage of the DRA is to ensure that students have adequately mobilized and developed cognitive structures so that the new information in the reading makes sense and can be accommodated in their cognitive structures. In the DRA model given here, a picture is used as the basis for both tapping what students already know and for developing their backgrounds on Mardi Gras and life in eighteenth century Italy.

In the next stage, Concept Development (1c), the teacher directly teaches vocabulary that the students must understand in order to answer the purpose-for-reading questions. Vocabulary should be taught directly and in an active mode by using strategies such as those described in the beginning of this chapter. Notice that the English teacher who designed the DRA on the Poe story used concrete representations (for *cask, catacomb,* and *carnival season*) and context

clues (for *impunity*) as priming strategies. Also notice that the Concept Development and Background of Experience stages of this lesson were accomplished simultaneously. Some readings lend themselves to this combination.

Immediately prior to Silent Reading, the students are given, or generate with teacher guidance, specific Purposes for Reading (1d). These purpose questions should not be large in number. One to three, well-focused questions will help students maintain their active engagement with the reading as they search for and write down the answers to the questions. The writing also develops the habit of note taking while reading, a strategy that facilitates independent study. The Purpose for Reading can also take the form of a challenge as opposed to direct questions. For example:

(Math) Disprove the following: Computers actually slow down the retail business.

(Social Studies) As you read, gather information that will allow you to assume the role of Andrew Jackson as he is interviewed by the press. Be prepared to

Greek Classical Heroes	Theseus	Perseus	Jason
Virtues			
Villain/Monsters			
Journeys			
Parents			
Help of Gods			
Conflict			

Chemical Elements of the Earth	Metals	Nonmetals
Good conductor?		
Malleable?		
Ductile?		

defend your decisions concerning removal of the Cherokee and Creek Indians to Oklahoma.

The Purpose for Reading can also take the form of a graphic organizer that the students would complete as they read. The graphic organizer shown previously for metals and nonmetals was the students' purpose for reading as they read a science chapter entitled, "Chemical Elements of the Earth."

In the next step of the DRA, Silent Reading (2), students read the material silently in order to satisfy the established purpose for reading. Immediately after the reading, a Discussion (3) of the purpose-for-reading questions occur. This can be an entire class discussion, or if the questions are of a high level of

Figures 5.3 and 5.4
Comparative
Feature Charts

difficulty, collaborative groups might first discuss, then reach a consensus with the entire class.

The next part of the DRA is Re-Reading (4). This can be a methodical reading of the entire selection again for different purposes for reading. For example, in an English class, it could be preparation for a dramatic reading. Re-Reading more often, however, involves the students in skimming the passage to discover additional concepts and principles. As with the Discussion phase of the DRA, this Re-Reading may take the form of independent work, small collaborative groups, and/or entire class discussion. In the sample DRA lesson plan given in this chapter, the students worked in pairs to complete the decision chart for Montresor's decisions. Then the entire class reached consensus and discussed generalized impressions of what qualifies as a *good* decision. In order to complete their charts, they referred back to the story, skimming to locate detail for the blocks.

The DRA concludes with an optional Follow-Up (5). This is an activity that might enrich or reinforce the learning that has taken place in the lesson. In the sample DRA, students engaged in a reinforcement activity that required them to apply their understanding of decision justification and evaluation to an actual decision they had made.

Notice how actively involved the students are within a DRA lesson format. Although the focus of this lesson type is on the processing of reading material, the students are also listening, speaking, and writing. Notice also the opportunities for the students to participate in collaborative learning.

Directed Reading Activity 5.2 (at end of chapter) is written for a middle school social studies class (Mason 1990). Your purpose for reading should now be to identify all the opportunities students are provided for listening, speaking, reading, and writing. Also notice the collaborative learning opportunities and the use of a graphic organizer for the Purpose for Reading section.

Directed-Reading-Thinking Activity

Another strategy that encourages active cognitive engagement on the part of the students is the Directed-Reading-Thinking Activity (DRTA), originally developed by Russell Stauffer (1969). The DRTA is a modification of the Purpose for Reading section of the DRA. Students use the title, illustrations, subheads, and sometimes the opening paragraph(s) of a piece of reading material to predict what they think the reading will be about and to generate their own purpose-for-reading questions. For example, students in a middle school science class who are about to read a chapter section on the moon, might be able to establish several purpose-for-reading questions by referring to the subhead, "Tides—the

Moon's Influence on the Oceans. Tapping their backgrounds of experience, students would then predict answers to their questions concerning how the moon affects the ocean tides. Students would read to verify their predictions. The ensuing Discussion would begin by asking students which of their predictions were accurate and which needed to be adapted.

An English teacher preparing to teach the short story, "The Monkey's Paw" by W.W. Jacobs, could ask the students to hypothesize what they believe the "monkey's paw" is and what it could be used for. Students would then read the first section to verify their predictions. Discussion could follow, where students could predict how the wish made on the monkey's paw would play itself out. Students would then continue to read the next section of the story in order to check their predictions.

Directed Inquiry Activity

The Directed Inquiry Activity (DIA), devised by Keith Thomas (1978), is an adaptation of the Directed-Reading-Thinking Activity (DRTA). In the DIA, students preview the reading selection as in a DRTA, but predict responses to six specific, inquiry questions: Who? What? When? Where? Why? and How? The teacher records all the student-generated responses under the appropriate inquiry category on the board or on a transparency. The teacher asks additional questions that require students to explain their predictions and to recognize interrelationships among questions. The students then read, as with the DRTA, to confirm or adapt their predictions.

This strategy is an attempt to actively involve students in generating their own purpose-for-reading questions, a skill they need to achieve successful reading during independent reading assignments. Notice that this variation of the Purpose for Reading can still be a part of the overall DRA lesson format that includes attention to background, concept development, silent reading, discussion, re-reading, and follow-up.

Independent Comprehension Strategy

All the strategies described thus far in this chapter on reading in the interactive classroom have been ones that require the teacher to be present to guide students through the active reading strategies. Students should also be taught to process reading independently for those occasions in secondary school, and certainly later in life, when there is no teacher to guide them in successfully interacting with reading material. Our goal should be to develop students who can independently engage in learning as a lifetime habit by asking the questions themselves. This requires teachers to instruct students in active cognitive strategies that will make them independent learners.

What independent reading strategies do you use? Do you ask yourself questions as teach-

ers do when they guide you through a reading? Do you deliberately relate what you already know to what you are reading?

The Independent Comprehension Strategy (ICS) (Loudermilk 1978) was designed to help students process reading material independent of teacher guidance. It consists of a series of questions that students ask themselves in order to tap their backgrounds and to set their own purpose-for-reading questions prior to reading. Students then read to verify their background ideas, to answer their purpose-for-reading questions, and to record additional information they learned (see Figure 5.5).

Step A., having students consider what they already know about a topic, is designed to mobilize available information in cognitive structures that are relevant to, and can play a subsuming role for, the new information in the reading material. These statements serve as cognitive questions also since, as they need, students will be marking each statement with:

+ The author(s) and I agree on this statement.

- The author(s) and I disagree on this statement. The author(s) believes . . .

0 This information is not discussed in this reading selection.

In Step B of the ICS, students decide what new information might be obtained from the specific reading selection. These questions become their purpose-for-reading questions as they read the content selection, channel-

---

Title of Reading _____

Topic of the Reading (my own words) _____

STEP A: What do I already know about this topic?

What I Know	Agreement (mark+, -, O, etc.)
1. _____	1. _____
2. _____	2. _____
3. _____	3. _____
4. _____	4 _____
ETC.	

STEP B: What questions might be answered in this reading?

Questions	Answers
1. _____	1. _____
2. _____	2. _____
3. _____	3. _____
4. _____	4 _____
ETC.	

STEP C: Other information I learned while reading.

1. _____
2. _____
3. _____
ETC.

Figure 5.5

Independent

Comprehension

Strategy

ing attention and guiding thinking.

In Step C of the ICS, students record additional information they learned while interacting with the text. Notice that all three of these parts of the ICS strategy require students to write as they read. Such writing promotes active cognitive engagement and facilitates recall of information.

Word Problems in Mathematics

Have you ever experienced the frustration of trying to comprehend mathematical word problems? Understanding what the writer is "giving" and "requesting" is prerequisite to applying any actual mathematical calculation. Word problems present a particularly challenging form of reading material because they are descriptions of everyday experiences that couch a mathematical problem to be identified and solved.

RQ4S2T: One interactive reading strategy that can be applied to word problems is the RQ4S2T reading formula (Singer and Donlan 1980). The mathematics teacher would present the following steps to students, then guide the students through the application of the steps to word problems. Through such guided practice, students become skilled in using this heuristic independently to break the code of word problems.

- *Read* the problem carefully. Review concepts by consulting a glossary; review explanation of

pertinent processes.
- *Question 1:* What facts are given?
- *Question 2:* What do I have to find out?
- *Question 3:* What shall I let "x" equal?
- *Question 4:* How shall I represent the other information?
- *Set up* the equation. Use the answers from steps 2–5 for the left and right components of the equation.
- *Solve* the problem.
- *Test* the answer by substituting the answer(s) in the equation.

Applied to the following word problem in algebra, the RQ4S2T formula would yield these results.

Word Problem: At 8 a.m., two planes leave the Baltimore-Washington International Airport. One plane travels north at 470 km/h; the other travels south at 490 km/h. What time will it be when the planes are 1440 km apart?

- *Read* the problem carefully. Review the concepts and formula for rate, time, and distance.
- *Question 1:* What facts are given?
  Two planes; both leave at 8 a.m.; one flies North and one flies South; one flies at 470km/h and the other flies at 490km/h.
- *Question 2:* What do I have to find out?
  What time will it be when the planes are 1440 km apart?
- *Question 3:* What shall I let "x" equal?

Let x = time.
- *Question 4:* How shall I represent the other information?
  First plane's distance
    $= 470x$
  Second plane's distance
    $= 490x$
- *Set up* the equation.
  $470x + 490x = 1440$
- *Solve* the equation.
  $470x + 490x = 1440$
      $960x = 1440$
         $x = 1.5$ hours
  8a.m. + 1.5 hours =
  9:30 a.m.
- *Test* the answer.
  $470 \times 1.5 +$
    $490 \times 1.5 = 1440$
  $705 + 735 = 1440$
    $1440 = 1440$

ReQuest Procedure: Another interactive reading procedure that has been used successfully by students to break the code of the word problem is Manzo's ReQuest Procedure (1969). Working on one sentence of the problem at a time, the students and the teacher alternate turns asking each other questions about the sentence. Consensus of understanding is reached through this questioning process so that the equation and calculations can then be finalized. Applied to the previous word problem, clarifying questions like the following may be asked of the first sentence in the problem.

- How many planes are involved?
- What time of day did the planes leave the airport?
- Did both planes leave at the same time?

This line of questioning would continue between students and teacher for each sentence to ensure comprehension of the information prior to development of the equation and calculation of the answer.

This ReQuest Procedure is particularly helpful with complex verbal mathematical problems because it dissects the crucial elements of the problem that must be comprehended if the problem is to be solved accurately.

Reader Response
Paul Armstrong (1990), a college professor, tells the story of a student who stopped by his office in search of another English professor whom the student had as an instructor in the previous semester. The student tells Armstrong that she needs to find the professor because:

> Professor X taught us this story in his class, and he told us what it meant, and now I have the same story in another class and I've forgotten what its interpretation is. I need to find him so he'll tell me because this other teacher won't (p. 125).

This scenario reflects much of the instruction that takes place in English (and other content area) classrooms. The students passively receive the teacher's interpretation of the reading.

Reader response, or reader-centered curriculum, is based on the theory that readers must be active during reading (interacting with the text), and that meaning evolves from transactions between the text and the reader's experience. Therefore, the text is not static.

Thus, though an author may have carefully chosen language and incident with quite specific references and impressions—perhaps readily understood by the author's immediate contemporaries—responses of audiences with variant experiences, especially those of another time and place, are subject to other environmental forces (Karolides 1992, p. 25).

This theory, first promulgated by Louise Rosenblatt (1938), undergirds a philosophy that encourages teachers to serve as facilitators to their students' comprehension. Instead of assuming the role of "font of all knowledge," the teacher is a guide to helping students develop a reflective stance to reading and the confidence in their own ability to interpret what an author has written.

In the English classroom, the teacher, acting on this theory, would present a literary work, then might ask the students to free-write their reactions to the work for five or 10 minutes. The teacher may focus the student's attention on a particular aspect of the work for reaction (e.g., a particular character or decision), or he or she may ask students to react to the entire piece. Students would then work in small groups to share their reactions, learn from each other as various perceptions are revealed, discuss similarities or differences in their reactions, and discuss the reasons for their different perceptions. Students are required to support their interpretations during these discussions and during any entire class discussion that may follow.

Some teachers who believe that students profit by being exposed to the interpretations of "published authorities," begin with a reader-response approach, then share what a published critic has written. Students are then encouraged to use critical thinking and respond to the published critic in light of their own beliefs. Through this procedure, students become more confident in their ability to be an "authority" on an author's work and less likely to automatically accept the interpretation of a published critic. Thus, they are more willing to become actively engaged in their reading.

SUMMARY

Reading is one of the most important language skills for learning content in the secondary school. The act of reading must actively engage the reader if comprehension is to take place. The strategies described in this chapter—vocabulary priming, graphic organizers, Directed Reading Activity, Directed-Reading-Thinking Activity, Directed Inquiry Activity, Independent

Comprehension Strategy, RQ4S2T and ReQuest procedure for word problems, and reader response—are designed to facilitate cognitive engagement on the part of the student. These strategies call for students to interact with the text and to interact with their peers and teacher in the classroom. They are interactive reading strategies that also call into play the other three language processing skills—listening, speaking, and writing.

BIBLIOGRAPHY

- Armstrong, P. "A Moment." In *What Is English?* by P. Elbow. New York: The Modern Language Association of America, 1990.
- Betts, E. *Foundations of Reading Instruction.* New York: American Book Company, 1946.
- Gutkoska, J. "State Champions." Baltimore, Md.: Towson State University, n.d. (photocopy).
- Hawk, P.P., and McLeod, N.P. "Graphic Organizer: An Effective Teaching Method." *Middle School Journal* 14 (1983): 20–22.
- Hawk, P.P., McLeod, N.P., and Jeane, K.L. "Graphic Organizers in Initial Learning and Retention." *California Journal of Educational Research* 2 (1981): 70–78.
- Karolides, N.J. "The Transactional Theory of Literature." In *Reader Response in the Classroom: Evoking and Interpreting Meaning in Literature*, N. Karolides, ed. White Plains, N.Y.: Longman Publishing Group, 1992.
- Loudermilk, G.N. "Vocabulary Priming." *Maryland English Journal* 15 (1976): 30–34.
- ___. Determining the Effectiveness of a Student-Centered Method of Instruction for Teaching an Independent Comprehension Strategy. Unpublished dissertation, 1978.
- Lyman, F.T. "The Responsive Classroom Discussion: The Inclusion of All Students." *Mainstreaming Digest* (1981): 109–12.
- Mason, V. "A Directed Reading Activity for Social Studies." Baltimore, Md.: Towson State University, 1990 (photocopy).
- Manzo, A.V. "The ReQuest Procedure." *Journal of Reading* 13 (1969): 123–26.
- McTighe, J. "Thinking About Adolescent Thinking." *The Early Adolescence Magazine* 1 (1986): 7–13.
- McTighe, J., and Lyman, F.T. "Cuing Thinking in the Classroom: The Promise of Theory-Embedded Tools." *Educational Leadership* 45 (1988): 18–24.
- Nelson-Herber, J. "Expanding and Refining Vocabulary in Content Areas." *Journal of Reading* 29 (1986): 626–33.
- Rosenblatt, L.M. *Literature As Exploration.* New York: D. Appleton-Century, Co., Inc., 1938.
- Singer, H., and Donlan, D. *Reading and Learning from Text.* Boston: Little, Brown, 1980.
- Stauffer, R. *Directing Reading Maturity As a Cognitive Process.* New York: Harper and Row, 1969.
- Thomas, K.J. "The Directed Inquiry Activity: An Instructional Procedure for Content Reading." *Reading Improvement* 15 (1978): 138–40.

Directed Reading Activity 5.1

Readiness

❋ *Motivation:*

"Today we begin reading a series of short stories and eventually a novel that have the main characters involved in making a number of decisions. Decisions are something we make every day. For example, already today I decided to wear this blue dress and not my red one. Six months ago, I decided to buy a Toyota. I could have decided to buy a Hyundai or a Honda. Now my decision about my dress may not have been very important, but my decision about the type of car I would buy was important. Think about an important decision you have made recently. Write for the next three minutes in your source book about that decision. Then we'll share those ideas."

Students write, then volunteers share their decisions. Ask each respondent what other choice might he or she have made.

"The characters in the first short story you will read also make some decisions—some very important decisions. Let me introduce you to those two characters now."

❋ *Background of Experience and Concept Development:*

Display the transparency of the picture of Fortunato and Montresor, the two characters in Edgar Allen Poe's "The Cask of Amontillado," in the catacombs. Fortunato is dressed as a clown for the Mardi Gras season.

Ask the students to:

- describe what they see in the picture;

- describe the attire of Fortunato (Ask: "Who knows what Mardi Gras is?" Show a Mardi Gras mask, and ask: "Why might Mardi Gras be called *carnival season*?")

- describe the attire of Montresor (Tell students about the attire of the eighteenth-century Italians.)

- hypothesize why the characters might be carrying torches. ("Where might they be?" Use the term *catacomb*. "What type of place might this be?" Draw students attention to the barrels and bottles and the skulls in the background of the picture. Relate the burial habits of the Italians in those days.)

To summarize, ask students to work with a partner and write definitions for the following concepts: *cask, catacomb, carnival season*. Reach a class consensus on definitions, and have students record these definitions in the vocabulary section of their notebooks.

"There is one additional word you need to understand before reading the story. The word is *impunity*. On the vocabulary transparency, are three examples of *impunity*. Read them, and with your partner, define *impunity*."

1. A woman robs a store, is caught and convicted, but due to a technicality during the trial, she is set free.

2. A student steals another student's CD, is caught by the vice-principal, but is allowed to go free.

3. A driver hits a child on a bicycle. The child dies. The driver is never caught.

Through an entire class discussion, reach a consensus on the definition of *impunity* (crime without punishment) and have students record the definition in their vocabulary notebooks.

❊ *Purpose for Reading:*
"As you read the story, 'The Cask of Amontillado,' write the answers to the questions that I am distributing."

1. What reason does Montresor give the reader for taking Fortunato to the catacombs? What reason does he give Fortunato for taking him to the catacombs?

2. How does Montresor get revenge?

Silent Reading

Students read the story silently; teacher encourages active reading for answers to the questions.

Discussion

Entire class discussion of the literal, purpose-for-reading questions.

Re-Reading

Students receive a decision chart (below) for "The Cask of Amontillado." After column headings are explained, the teacher leads the class through Fortunato's decisions, rationales, and evaluation. In pairs, students will then complete the chart for Montresor's decisions. Finally, an entire class discussion validates the chart responses made by the pairs of students and determines what qualifies as a *good decision*. *Logical* and *fair* are operationally defined in terms of rational arguments and respect of others involved.

Decision Chart

Character	What decisions are made by the character?	What is character's justification for for this decision?	Is the decision a good one? (fair? logical?)
Fortunato			
Montresor			

Follow-Up

Students use their original source book entries about a major decision each of them has made. They write an explanation of their rationale for the decision and evaluate it in terms of being *logical* and *fair*.

(End of Lesson)

Directed Reading Activity 5.2

SOCIAL STUDIES-AMERICAN HISTORY

GRADE 6

Readiness

❋ *Motivation:*

"Who has lived somewhere in the United States other than here in Maryland? How was life different there? Why?"

❋ *Tapping Background of Experience:*

"Today we will be reading about the different life-styles of the New England versus the Southern Colonists as we continue our study of early American History. Let's review which states made up each of these areas."

❋ *Concept Development:*

Pair students for Think-Pair-Share. Invite pairs to read the following sentences and to formulate a definition of *commerce*.

1. President Clinton and business leaders visited Japan recently to discuss ways in which commerce between Japan and the United States could be increased.

2. Due to the increase in imports and exports, commerce has increased by 20 percent in recent years.

3. The Port of Baltimore has been a major commerce center for centuries.

Entire class discussion is then used to reach consensus on the definition, which students record in their social studies vocabulary notebooks.

Teacher writes *seaport* on the board and instructs students to close their eyes, listen, and image:

> You are to imagine you are on a Sunday afternoon ride with your parents. It is a warm and humid day, and the windows are rolled down in the car. There is a breeze hitting your face and blowing through your hair. You arrive at your destination. This town is located on the water. As you get out of the car, you can see a ship pull up to the docks. The sailors jump off and begin to unload the cargo, boxes, and barrels from the ship. This town is a seaport. Now open your eyes and write your definition of seaport.

Pairs collaborate on a definition, then class discussion results in a consensus definition that students record in their notebooks.

❋ *Purpose for Reading:*

"As you read the handout I distribute, you are to contrast the life of a New England colonist to the life of a southern colonist. Use the chart (on the following page) to record your responses."

Silent Reading

Students read silently and record responses in the following chart.

Contrasting Colonists' Life-Styles

	New England Colonist	Southern Colonist
Major occupations		
Type of commerce		
Style of home		
Forms of education		
Dress		

Discussion

Entire class discusses chart information.

Re-Reading

With your partner, use the text, your chart information, and the pictures in the reading to formulate a response to this question:

What major factor contributed to these differences in life-style between the colonists in New England and the colonists of the South?

Entire class discussion results in the generalization that geography—surroundings and conditions—was the major factor.

Follow-Up

"Assume the role of an 11- or a 12-year-old who is living in the colonies. Half the room will be New Englanders and half Southerners. You have a pen pal in the other area with whom you communicate regularly. Write a letter to him or her and talk about your day. Keep in mind the geographical surroundings and therefore your life-style. You will exchange letters tomorrow."

(End of Lesson)

Practice

1. Select a reading for your content area and design a graphic organizer that students can use to facilitate their comprehension of it.

2. Using one of the Directed Reading Activities (DRAs) in this chapter, describe how you could adapt the purpose-for-reading concept for a Directed-Reading-Thinking Activity (DRTA). Do the same for a directed inquiry activity (DIA).

3. Select a text you are currently reading for a college class or using with a group of secondary students. Apply the Independent Comprehension Strategy (ICS) to your independent reading of this material. How does this compare or contrast to the study method you use?

4. Draft a Directed Reading Activity for your content area. Give particular attention to vocabulary instruction that involves the students in constructing the meaning of the vocabulary words through the vocabulary priming process. Share the lesson with a member of your methods class or teach it to your students.

5. Mathematics Teachers: Apply the RQ4S2T formula to a word problem. Does it help you? Teach it to a group of math students. Ask them for their reaction.

6. English Teachers: Present a poem to a group of students via the reader-response technique. Reflect on the different message you are conveying to your students about control of interpretation of the meaning of the poem.

CLASSROOM CARRY-OVER

Here's how I plan to use what I just earned about reading in the interactive classroom.

_____
_____
_____
_____
_____
_____
_____
_____
_____
_____
_____
_____
_____
_____
_____
_____
_____
_____
_____
_____
_____
_____
_____
_____
_____
_____
_____
_____
_____
_____

CHAPTER 6

Writing in the Interactive Classroom

How do you use writing activities to encourage learning?

READINESS

Think about all the informal writing you have done in the past few days, that is, writing in which you engaged for personal reasons rather than writing a finished product shared with a large audience. Then list at least three types of informal writing you have done and reasons why you engaged in these types of writing.

1. _____
   _____
   _____

2. _____
   _____
   _____

3. _____
   _____
   _____

Now, think about how a teacher could use similarly informal writing activities as a way to initiate a class session. For instance, you may write reminders to yourself about things you need to do during the day; as a teacher, you could have students write "reminders" to themselves about procedures they previously learned on which to build understanding of new material. You might write questions you want to ask when you are on the phone talking to your ad-visor, the registrar, or your insurance agent; as a teacher, you might ask students to write a list of questions they still have about material previously presented for which they should listen to answers during the new class session. Make a list describing how each of the items you provided in the previous list might be adapted for use in initiating a lesson plan .

1. _____
   _____
   _____

2. _____
   _____
   _____

3. _____
   _____
   _____

Purpose for Reading

The reading material in this chapter will help you answer the following questions: What does the phrase "writing-to-learn" mean? How can teachers use writing at the beginning of a class session, during a lesson, or at the end of class in order to facilitate students' efforts to learn course content and to make sense of that content in a personal way? Why does writing work as a learning/teaching tool in the interactive classroom?

READING MATERIAL

The Writing-to-Learn Process and the Value of Writing to Learn

This chapter is organized somewhat differently than the chapters you have already read. Because you have been writing as you have read the previous material, and because you will be writing as you read this chapter, at the end of this chapter, you will be asked to process all your experiences with writing so that, inductively, you will be able to determine a definition for "writing to learn" and you will be able to articulate its value in the interactive classroom. Also, because writing-to-learn strategies are used in tandem with listening, reading, and speaking activities, you will find, at the end of this chapter, a list of possible types of writing that you might ask students to attempt, all of which have many generic applications.

Using Writing to Begin a Class

Think about a teacher who asked you to write as a way to

initiate class. What did you write about? What happened to you as you wrote? Why do you suppose the teacher selected a writing activity? What was the value of the writing to you as student and to her as teacher?

Now that you have your tapped background of experience related to the idea of using writing as a way to help students ready themselves for learning, read the following scenarios about teachers using writing in just this way. As you do, make a list of the types of writing activities presented and write about why you think the teacher used the specific strategy as a means to start the lesson.

Scenarios: Writing to Learn At the Beginning of Class

Scenario 1: Ms. Smith, an English teacher, has the following assignment written on the board for her students to tackle as they enter the classroom:

> In your reading log, write about what event marked the arrival of spring for you as a young child and what events herald its arrival for you at your current age.

Later, Ms. Smith introduces the novel *Dandelion Wine* by Ray Bradbury by discussing with students their "rites of spring" and how they relate to those of the main character in the book, which is about one rather magic summer in his life.

Identify the following for Scenario 1.

1. Writing strategy
2. Reason for using strategy

Scenario 2: Mr. Connolly tells his music class to open their journals and to write about the type of mood they would want to create in a piece of music designed to celebrate the grandeur of the Rocky Mountains and a natural phenomenon such as the Grand Canyon. He also asks the students to brainstorm a list of musical instruments they might use in trying to create those sounds and moods and then to explain why they selected these instruments and sounds.

Identify the following for Scenario 2:

1. Writing strategy
2. Reason for using strategy

Scenario 3: Ms. Pullman opens her government class by saying, "While I take attendance, in your day books, I want you to *be* our representative to the House of Representatives. Based on our discussion yesterday, make a list of "things to do" for a typical day on which the House of Representatives meets."

Identify the following for Scenario 3.

1. Writing strategy
2. Reason for using writing strategy

Scenario 4: Mr. Greer shows his art class reproductions of two cathedrals, one from the late Roman period and one from the latter part of the Gothic period. He asks

them to take notes for several minutes on the differences they observe in the architecture and then to brainstorm a list of the technical problems builders must have had to tackle in order to develop the features that distinguish the Gothic construction from the earlier one.

Identify the following for Scenario 4.

1. Writing strategy
2. Reason for using writing strategy

Scenario 5: When students arrive in Ms. Green's biology class, they find the following circled words on large pieces of newsprint paper that are hanging from the wall at various locations in the classroom: *food chain, water cycle, ecosystem, oxygen cycle*. As soon as the bell rings, she says, "Row One, go to *food chain* and create a web of all the associations and bits of information you have, collectively, for that term. Each person should contribute at least two items, but remember, you may build off of a word someone else contributes. Row Two, do the same for *water cycle*; Row Three, the same for *ecosystem*; and Row Four, work with *oxygen cycle*. You have five minutes." When the students are back in their seats, she asks them to look at the various webs and then helps them, as a class, generate a list of questions they have about the various terms and their relationships. She then uses their responses in presenting a lesson about these concepts, building on their existing knowledge.

Identify the following for Scenario 5.

1. Writing strategy
2. Reason for using strategy

Scenario 6: Mr. Wise tells his shop class that it is going to begin a unit on types of metals. He asks each student to write about that topic for three minutes. He calls "time," and instructs students to exchange papers. They must then react in writing to what their partner has written. The papers are then returned to their authors and read. At that point, the teacher begins the class discussion by asking students to volunteer information or ideas from their papers.

Identify the following for Scenario 6.

1. Writing strategy
2. Reason for using writing strategy

Scenario 7: Mr. Brown begins his literature class by having students, in groups of four, share entries completed for homework in their dialectical or double-entry journals, journals in which they write while doing their reading (Berthoff 1981, 1987). Students divide their paper in half. On the left side of the page, they jot down illustrative quotations and facts about characters, setting, or plot events that strike them for some reason; they are free to draw pictures, make webs of related words, and otherwise vary the format. On the right hand side, they write about why they made that entry, "cooking those ideas" (Vaughan 1990) by jotting down their questions and comments about the text in a reader-response based approach to the literature. Mr. Brown asks each group to generate one question they had about the reading, which is passed to another group for response.

Identify the following for Scenario 7.

1. Writing strategy
2. Reason for using strategy

Looking at your lists of specific strategies and reasons for using them, try in Figure 6.1, to match each activity with the purpose(s) for its use.

In the first English class, students are recalling personal experiences (the phrase for doing so that is often used in education texts is "tapping prior knowledge" or "tapping background of experience") that will help them better relate to the piece of literature they will be reading. In the music class, students have been set a "problem" that a composer might have to tackle, and they must generate possible solutions based on their knowledge of how various instruments sound. In the government class, students are role-playing in writing as a way to review a prior discussion about the responsibilities of a member of the House of Representatives. In the art class, students must make careful observations as they compare and contrast new material to old, and then they attempt to predict some of the

DIRECTIONS: Match each activity in Column A with a purpose (or purposes) in Column B.

Activity: Column A	Purpose: Column B
a. Write about a personal experience (English class).	1. Review.
b. Write about how to apply knowledge as an expert would (music class).	2. Develop readiness for reading by examining relevant personal experience.
c. Develop a list of things to do (based on discussion in government class).	3. Develop observation skills.
d. Record observations and hypothesize (art class).	4. Develop skill in creating hypotheses.
e. Collaboratively tap prior knowledge through web or sharing writing (biology and industrial arts).	5. Provide information teacher may use to diagnose knowledge level.
f. Develop questions to guide future learning (biology class).	6. Develop social skills of cooperation and sharing.

(Answers: a–2; b–1,4,5; c–1,5; d–1,3,4; e–1,5,6; f–1,5,6)

technological advances made in the Gothic period from those observations. In both the biology and shop classes, students are collecting and tapping prior knowledge, both individually—and collaboratively—as a springboard for learning new material. In the literature class, students are writing to provide themselves with a written record of their response to a text.

Now, what is the value of using writing in these ways?

1. Students' attention is focused on the topic. They

Figure 6.1

Writing to Learn:

Strategies and

Reasons for Their Use

come into a classroom carrying a great deal of emotional and cognitive "baggage" from other classes and experiences in the halls, and the writing serves as a way to help them get ready to participate in the class at hand by providing a focus for their attention. Without such attention, little learning is likely to occur. Engaging in writing at the beginning of class has a settling effect on students.

2. As they write, students are activating their minds. As they reflect on prior knowledge and their own experiences, they create a base on which the teacher can build in presenting new information or new processes to them.

3. The actual process of writing increases students' active mental involvement. As they write, they must be intellectually engaged in the task or no words will be forthcoming. As each word appears on a page, students reflect on what word will follow. And, in the act of writing, students commit themselves. The words stay on the paper for immediate and future reference. Writing requires students to organize their thoughts, to clarify meanings and relationships in order to articulate them on the paper—in short, to *think*.

Using Writing in the Middle of a Class

Have you ever had a teacher stop class and ask you to take "time out" from the lesson activities to write about what you had been doing or to predict how the lesson might continue

to unfold? Try to answer the following questions in your own mind; perhaps you want to write about them in your reading log or perhaps you would prefer to discuss them with a friend: What did the teacher ask you to do? What happened to you as you wrote? What was the value of the writing from your perspective as a student? What was the value of the writing from the teacher's point of view? Why do you think the teacher chose to use a writing activity?

If you have never had the type of experience described in the previous paragraph, try to imagine such a scenario for a class you have experienced and describe ways the instructor might have used writing to engage students in the lesson.

Now that you have considered your own experience or have thought about the possible reasons for stopping a lesson to have students write about what they have been learning, read the following scenarios that describe teachers using writing during a lesson. As you read, take notes about the types of writing activities the teachers use and then write about why these teachers asked their students to engage in these activities.

Scenarios: Writing in the Middle of a Class

Scenario 1: Ms. Lester feels confident that her Algebra I students understand the process they have been reviewing for the graphing of linear equalities. Before she begins the next segment of the lesson, she says, "I think you

all have a good grasp of what we have been doing. In your notebook, take a minute to write out a generalized list of the steps we have been following so far. Then, write about how you think that procedure will need to be changed or adapted if we move into the graphing of linear inequalities."

Scenario 2: The students in Mr. Timothy's seventh grade history class have been engaged in a lively discussion of the issues involved as the colonies moved closer to independence. But, students are starting to ignore the historical facts. So, he says, "Take out your journals and do a Venn diagram that describes the three key issues at this time of crisis and the stance taken by the colonists and by the Crown on these issues."

Scenario 3: After reading and discussing the "Note Cultural" in their French texts that describes the French educational system, Mr. Amatman asks his students to write for two minutes about their reactions to what they have read and to then write the rough draft in their notebooks of a letter to their assigned pen pal that describes their perceptions of French schooling and to ask any questions they may have about these perceptions.

Scenario 4: After her demonstration on making crepes, Ms. Pennell asks students to write down in their notebooks the three most important points they must keep in mind as they strive to create their own perfect crepes. Then, in their work groups, she tells students to synthesize their lists to create posters that they will hang over their work stations for reference as they begin to cook.

Scenario 5: Ms. Benson has just finished part of a lesson on defensive strategies in basketball. She asks students to write variations on the type of riddle that begins, "I have X, Y, and Z characteristics. Who am I?" ("I" in these riddles will be a defensive strategy.) She then takes a few minutes to read some of the "riddles" and to generate responses before moving into the next section of the lesson during which students actually practice the strategies.

How did the previous writing activities students to engage them to learn lesson content more effectively?

1. In the Algebra I class, students generalize steps in a procedure, indicating their comprehension of a relatively complex cognitive task by using their own words to do so. Then, once they put the procedures into their own words, they predict their applicability to a new situation. The writing process helps them connect new information to old, acting as a bridge from one portion of the lesson to the next.

2. Students also demonstrate their understanding and comprehension of key issues and the comparative stances on those issues by doing the Venn diagram exercise in the history class. As the teacher analyzes those diagrams, he can determine whether or not the students understand why these issues are of such impor-

tance in determining historic events about to take place. Doing the diagram also forces the students to be at least somewhat objective in considering why the Crown felt itself justified in the stance it took against the Colonists, thus helping the students to recognize that there are two sides to most disputes.

3. In the French class, the teacher uses writing as a way to help students personalize information found in the text. As they discuss their reactions, the teacher will have the basis for interesting conversations that involve skills of comparison and contrast. Asking the students to draft a note to a pen pal forces the students to commit themselves to their perceptions and to explain them as well as possible to an audience not familiar with the U.S. educational system.

4. In the home economics class, the teacher asks students to write as a way to focus on main ideas. As the work groups strive to create one poster, they are also developing skills of sequencing and synthesis.

5. And, in the physical education class, the teacher is allowing students to review new material, to put it into their own words, thus demonstrating to her whether or not they comprehend it, prior to asking them to apply that material.

Now, generalize in writing the value of the writing activities these teachers have used in the middle of their lesson plans. Compare your list to the following one.

1. The writing increases

the number of students who are mentally engaged in the class at any given point in time and thus increases the number of students who can actually engage in discussion.

2. Writing serves to help each student clarify personal thoughts about and responses to the class content. If students can put information into their own words or relate it to their own experience, they comprehend the material in a way that goes beyond just memorization of facts and processes.

3. Through writing, students discover both what they know and what they do not know as they try to put that knowledge into their own words. If the students recognize that there are points of confusion during the processing of the writing, the students have motivation for learning.

4. As the teacher looks at students' writings, or as he or she processes responses with the group, the teacher receives feedback about the students' progress in learning the material and thus has a basis on which to make decisions about where to go next with the lesson. The teacher can evaluate students' understanding and can reteach and correct misconceptions before they are "learned" as fact.

Using Writing at the Close of a Class Period

Think (or free-write briefly) about a lesson you enjoyed for some reason, and then imagine what type of writing the teacher of that lesson could have incorporated at the end to help you practice with the material you had been learning. Now, here are some examples of how teachers in a variety of classrooms use writing activities in closing their lessons. Read through the scenarios and make a list of writing strategies that the teachers use to help bring the class to closure. Generalize, either in writing or by discussing with a partner, about why the writing helps the students and teacher process the lesson at the end of the class.

Scenario 1: Ms. Miller tells her psychology class, "Before the bell rings for dismissal, write down what you think the key concepts are that we covered today in this session on dreams and sleep behavior." After students do so, she displays selected responses on the board, correcting any misconceptions and reinforcing those ideas she had been trying to emphasize.

Scenario 2: Mr. Winner concludes his explanation of how to conjugate regular *ir* verbs in French by saying, "Susan is absent today. Each of you write her a note describing the process we have been discussing and giving her examples from this list of new vocabulary words, all of which are regular *ir* verbs."

Scenario 3: After concluding his introductory lesson on ecosystems, Mr. Moss asks his biology students to write out three questions they have about ecosystems and then tells them to find the answers to these as they read the assigned text chapter for homework.

Scenario 4: Ms. Blue asks her health students to write her notes, anonymously, at the end of her lesson on nutrition answering the following questions: "What did you like about class today? What did you dislike? What did I do that was effective in helping you learn? What did you find to be ineffective?" She collects these notes and uses them in preparing the next lesson in the unit.

Scenario 5: Ms. Clemmens concludes her lesson on transposing from one key to another in her music-theory class by asking students to write out the procedures they should follow. She has students exchange papers and correct and add to each other's outlines.

Scenario 6: Mr. Plimpton has just collected a quiz from his geometry students. He asks them to write in their geometry logs on the following topics: What do you expect to receive on the quiz? What were the hardest problems? What was the easiest part? What could you or I have done to improve your performance on this quiz? What do you need to study and learn better for the unit test?

Scenario 7: After he finishes a presentation on norm groups, Mr. Avery gives each of his sociology students a marker and invites them to do a class cluster on that topic as a way to reinforce the concepts and interconnections discussed during the lesson.

Scenario 8: Mr. England wraps up a class discussion focused on the character of Hester in *The Scarlet Letter* by having students individually write a one-syllable word that describes her, then two syllables (either two one-syllable words or one two-syllable word), then three syllables, then four, then five. At that point, he asks for volunteers to share their "lines," and he creates on the board a poem, which emerges as a diamond-shape, moving from one syllable through five and back to one, capturing all that the class has said about the complex personality of Hester.

9. Ms. Smythe ends a class session on Moslem art by having students complete three sentences, based on this structure: "I used to think/feel/know _____ about Moslem art, but now I think/feel/know _____ about it."

What writing strategies did you list as you read about these teachers and their efforts to bring their lessons to closure? You should have the following items: list of key concepts, note to classmate describing procedure explained in class, questions students have after being introduced to new material, personal response to the teacher's strategies in class, outline of procedures that is exchanged and corrected by a partner, personal response to a quiz and analysis of student's strengths and weaknesses in taking it, and a collaborative, visual review of major concepts through two strategies—the class cluster and the class poem.

Why did the teachers use these various strategies? In the psychology class, the teacher received feedback through the writing about what students perceived to be important in the lesson and about concepts that continued to confuse students. Now she will be able to plan her next lesson more effectively, and the students have had an opportunity to "own" the concepts by using their own language to explain them. The same reasons hold for the French class and the music class. In each case, as the students try to explain a procedure, they and the teacher will be able to recognize points at which their understanding of that process is still hazy. The students can then ask questions, and the teacher can plan reinforcement activities more easily once problem areas are pinpointed through the writing process. In the biology class, the writing of questions serves as a "readiness for reading" activity. The students, having generated their own questions, should be motivated to read to find the answers. The health teacher and the geometry teachers both allow students to feel some ownership for the class by asking for feedback on their instructional techniques. The teachers can then improve their instruction, making it more suited to the learning styles of their students. And, in the case of the geometry class, students should begin to realize that they as well as the teacher have a responsibility for analyzing their own progress and taking steps to improve their performance as a result of that analysis. Finally, in the sociology and English classes, the collaborative efforts should help

reinforce the material discussed in class, should help students focus on important aspects of the class session, and should help demonstrate to them the power of collaboration in reviewing. Now, based on your understanding of learning theory and on the material presented in Chapter 2, create a list, similar to the lists found at the end of the first two sections in this chapter, in which you generalize about how these writing activities relate to learning theory. Compare your list to the one that follows.

1. Summarizing key concepts informs students about the extent of their knowledge and thus can serve as motivation to learn more.

2. Asking students to ask questions based on their increased knowledge base reinforces the fact that learning is an ongoing process. The questions serve as a guide either for the teacher to plan the next step of the unit sequence or for the students to focus their independent learning.

3. As the teacher processes this type of writing, the teacher becomes informed about what students did and did not learn, what they still need to learn, what needs to be retaught, and what is well grasped.

4. Having students outline a process in their own words informs both students and teachers about the accuracy of the students' perceptions of that process. Also, the writing serves to force the students to verbalize in their own personal language concepts that otherwise remain locked in the code

of the language of the discipline.

5. Using writing to summarize the class session facilitates and nurtures students' writing skills and their ability to use language to communicate their increased understanding and knowledge.

6. Asking students to write about how the class session has changed what they think, feel, and/or believe offers them practice in metacognition, or "thinking about their thought processes," and thus fosters self-awareness.

7. Any of these strategies can be used to increase the lines of communication between teacher and students, which contributes to students' perception that the teacher cares about them and about making the class a comfortable, effective learning environment, which, in turn, increases motivation and self-esteem.

8. The writing provides a *permanent record* from which students can study in the future.

The Value of Using Writing as a Learning Tool

Having read about specific writing strategies teachers use to help students prepare for a lesson, to process a lesson while it is progressing, and to help students synthesize a lesson, try to write one sentence in which you generalize about the power of using writing as a learning tool in planning for student-centered instruction. Now read these concluding remarks to determine if you understand the term "writing as a learning tool" as we have been using it.

Defining "Writing as a Learning Tool"

Whether the writing has occurred at the beginning, middle, or end of the class session, in all the scenarios presented in this chapter, the writing has served as a learning tool because it has been designed "to help students gain authority over their knowledge and gain independence in using it" (Bruffee 1984). The writing provides a record of student thought that teachers can use to determine if students actually caught on to whatever the content, process, or main idea of the lesson was supposed to be, thus allowing for teachers to individualize future instruction (Moffett and Wagner 1983).

The scenarios in this chapter demonstrate what researchers such as Emig (1977) or Berthoff (1981) have found in studying writers at work. While writing, writers practice:

1. higher level thinking skills of reflection (What are the implications? Why is this important to me?)

2. clarifying (Do I understand this enough to put it in my own words?)

3. projecting (Given this information, what do I predict will happen in another situation?)

4. organizing (What comes first? Last?)

5. analyzing (What is important here?)

6. interpreting (What does this mean?).

Also, the writing described in the scenarios within this chapter provides students with permanent histories of their search for knowledge and understanding. As Britton (1970), Olson (1977), and Odell (1980) note, one of the most important reasons why writing assists the learning process is that communicating in writing requires a degree of commitment not demanded in speaking.

While they write, students are actively engaged in all three of Bruner's "modes of knowing." Bruner (1973) states that individuals can learn through their kinesthetic experiences, through their visual experiences, and through reflective experiences. Writers see their thoughts flow onto the page while their hands traverse it, and they are constantly thinking about those words and their implications, reflecting on how they have arrived at that point on the page and considering where the words will lead them next.

Perhaps most importantly, the writing provides the type of practice with content required for mastery of it (Bower and Hilgard 1981). And, the types of writing activities outlined here also serve as a way for teachers to evaluate the learning that should be taking place as students engage in the types of student-centered strategies discussed elsewhere in this book!

In instances where students work together to produce a piece of writing, the effort must be a truly collaborative one rather than merely cooperative. As students struggle to produce *one* set of words on the page, they must come to consensus in a way they may not otherwise be forced to do if only a discussion follows the collaborative efforts.

Writing Activities from A to Z

Frequently, students have been conditioned to expect that writing in a classroom setting means either filling in blanks on duplicating masters or writing five-paragraph themes. As you attempt to engage students actively in the learning process through the use of writing as a learning tool, you might want to refer to the following list of possibilities for forms of writing students can use to help them practice with a variety of genres and to increase their understanding of the options available in real life.

Also: If you are using writing as a learning tool, keep in mind that these writing options should be given as "draft only" activities. The list is designed to provide alternatives to the typical instructions of "Write About . . . ," "Make a list of . . . ," or "Brainstorm in writing . . . ."

A. Aphorisms, anagrams, autobiography (real or fictional), advertisements, advice columns, analogies, argumentative essays, analyses, applications

B. Biography, bumper stickers, billboards

C. Confessions (real or fictional), children's stories and poetry, cartoons, commercials, captions (for pictures and cartoons), comic strips, cumulative stories, classified ads, comparison/contrasts

D. Dramatic monologues (written, recorded, or improvised), diaries, dictation, dialogues, dialogue journals (See Nancie Atwell's *In the Middle* for a discussion of variations of this strategy.)

E. Editorials, eulogies, euphemisms, epitaphs, epigrams, essays

F. Fiction, film scripts, "found" poetry, fill-in-the-blank items

G. Graffiti, goals, greeting cards, grocery lists

H. Humorous pieces, haiku

I. Interior monologues, imitations of forms, interviews, insults

J. Journals, jokes, jump-rope jingles

K. Kernel sentences and expansions

L. Light verse, limericks, light essays (e.g., E.B. White, Thurber), let's pretend, letters (to the editor, to a family member, to a loved one, or to an enemy), lists of all sorts

M. Metaphors, monographs, magazine articles, mobiles

N. Newspapers, news stories, notebook jottings

O. Observation logs, observation papers, onomatopoeia, one-act plays, outlines

P. Profiles, portraits, photo essays, parodies, poetry (free form or structured), protest songs, posters, propaganda, petitions, puppet shows, paragraphs, paragraph frames, persuasive speeches

Q. Questions, query letters

R. Rhymed verse, reminis-

cences, research, recordings, riddles, raps

S. Sketches, slide-tape scripts, stream of consciousness pieces, satires, stories, sound tapes, songs, speeches, sentence starters

T. Telegrams, TV scripts

U. Underground newspaper stories, unrhymed verse

V. Vitae, verse, vocabulary stories, Venn diagrams

W. Westerns, walking-tour scripts, word-picture paragraphs, word problems for math/science/economics, want ads

X. "Xeroxing" (imitations of others' works)

Y. Young adult fiction/poetry

Z. Zany anecdotes, zippy "comebacks," zodiac stories, zeugmas

Do's and Don'ts for Using Writing as a Learning Tool

Are there some do's and don'ts for using writing to learn strategies? Yes!

Do's for Using Writing as A Learning Tool

- The teacher should structure writing activities to

1. help students integrate their past knowledge and experience with new knowledge;

2. encourage personal exploration of concepts and ideas;

3. encourage comprehension of processes and ideas in a personally meaningful way;

4. allow students to practice with the entire spectrum of discourse; that is, students need not always write one-page summaries but can use diagrams, posters, riddles, questions, poems, and an infi-

nite variety of formats in which to explore their understandings;

5. enhance the development of collaboration;

6. provide an opportunity to practice role playing, for stepping into the shoes of another, or to use language as sharply as possible to facilitate communication with another person;

7. provide options—not all students will respond equally well to any given writing activity; and

8. reflect on major objectives and their personal relevance and to assess personal progress and development in the content area.

- The teacher should write with the students, demonstrating a belief in the value of writing as a learning tool.
- And, the teacher should provide time for processing the writing, whether through class discussions, peer response, or individual teacher feedback on the writing.

Don'ts for Using Writing as A Learning Tool

- The teacher should not grade or evaluate writing generated through strategies previously described for grammar, spelling, mechanics, and usage. Keep in mind that this sort of writing, while it may lead to a first draft of a more formal type of written product, is *not* meant to be evaluated as a finished piece; students are not writing *final products*. Entries in learning logs, for instance, can be taken through the steps of the writing process, which is usually said to include prewriting, drafting, revising, editing, and publishing; but the initial entry is not a final product and can *not* be read in that spirit. The reason for using writing as outlined in this chapter is that, "Much beyond the English classroom, writing supports more complex thinking and learning about the subjects that students are expected to learn" (Applebee and Langer 1987, p. 151).

- Teachers should not establish too many restrictions within which students must operate when writing. For the most part, the strategies described in this chapter are variations on the concept of "free writing," meaning that the writer should feel free to follow the flow of words wherever it wants to go, and that the writer should allow the writing to find its own form. If a student starts by trying to do a "web," but ends up using some other form of graphic organizer or an outline or just a freely written paragraph, that is perfectly acceptable, as long as the writing helps the student in the learning process.

SUMMARY

Writing in the classroom has traditionally been, and still is, used as an evaluative tool. Teachers ask students to write research papers, critical analyses, book reports, and essays in order to determine if students possess and can use specific information (Applebee and Langer 1987). Given that goal, it makes sense, then, for the teacher to be the primary, usually the only, audience for the writing, and the teacher typically responds to a "finished" product with a grade and perhaps some commentary about the organization, style, or mechanics of the piece. However, now that you have read about and analyzed teachers' use of writing as an instructional tool, perhaps you can begin to see the value of incorporating writing activities into your classroom in ways that not only evaluate, but *facilitate* learning. When students write, they have to be active in their learning. When students write, they have a basis for speech and they can create a record of others' speech. When students write while they read, they process information more actively and thus enhance their ownership of the text—and they create texts to which they, and others, can later refer. Writing-to-learn strategies provide a measure of accountability in an interactive classroom. They allow teachers to monitor students' thinking processes by reflecting on their written products. Writing-to-learn strategies thus become a springboard for future interaction as students revise their understanding and reshape their thoughts into words on the page.

BIBLIOGRAPHY

- Atwell, N. *In the Middle: Writing, Reading, and Learning with Adolescents.* Portsmouth, N.H.: Boyton/Cook Publishers, 1987.

- Applebee, A., and Langer, J. *How Writing Shapes Thinking.* Urbana, Ill.: National Council of Teachers of English, 1987.

- Bertoff, A. *The Making of Meaning: Metaphors, Models, and Maxims for Writing Teachers.* Portsmouth, N.H.: Boynton Cook, 1981.

- ___. "Dialectical Notebooks and the Audit of Meaning." In *The Journal Book*, ed. T. Fulwiler. Portsmouth, N.H.: Boyton Cook, 1987.

- Bower, G.H., and Hilgard, E.R. *Theories of Learning.* 5th edition. Englewood Cliffs, N.J.: Prentice-Hall, 1981.

- Britton, J.N. *Language and Learning.* London: Penguin Books, 1970.

- Bruffee, K. "Collaborative Learning and the 'Conversation of Mankind.'" *College English* 46 (1984): 635–52.

- Bruner, J. *The Relevance of Education.* New York: W.W. Norton, 1973.

- Emig, J. "Writing as a Mode of Learning." *College Composition and Communication* 28 (1977): 122–28.

- Moffett, J., and Wagner, B.J. *Student-Centered Language Arts and Reading, K–13: A Handbook for Teachers*, 3rd edition. Boston: Houghton Mifflin, 1983.

- Olson, D.R. "From Utterance to Text: The Bias of Speech in Thought and Action." *Harvard Educational Review* 47 (1977): 257–81.

- Odell, L. "The Process of Writing and the Process of Learning." *College Composition and Communication* 32 (1980): 42–50.

- Vaughan, C.L. "Knitting Writing: The Double-Entry Journal." In *Coming to Know: Writing to Learn in the Intermediate Grades*, ed. N. Atwell. Portsmouth, N.H.: Boyton Cook, 1990. 69–75.

Practice

1. Practice developing plans that use writing as a learning tool at the beginning, middle, and end of class.

   • Think about a lesson you might teach. Create two possible ways you might use a writing activity to start this class. One of these options should be one that asks students to work together, as the biology and shop teachers did. When you have your list, share it with a friend. Ask the friend to tell you what purpose the writing activity serves, and, if possible, the type of thinking your writing activities demand of the students. Try one of the activities yourself. Did it work in the ways you anticipated? What changes will you make before you use the idea in a classroom? Try one of your partner's activities and talk about how you felt while you were writing to give your partner a sense of how students might respond to the assignments. Ask your partner to do the same for you.

   • Go back to the lesson taught by Ms. Jones in Chapter 1. Write down two ways in which the teacher could use a writing-to-learn activity in the middle of the procedures section to enhance the lesson plan. Create at least one strategy that involves students in collaborative writing and learning. Share your ideas with a partner or friend. Does your partner think the writing will accomplish the same objectives you had in mind? Try one of the activities yourself. Did it work as you had hoped?

   • Look back over a lesson plan you have already completed. Brainstorm a number of ways you could use writing to strengthen your closure section. Include both individual and collaborative strategies. Share your ideas with a partner, asking him or her for advice about what to keep and what to change in your plan. Select what you think is your best strategy and tell your partner why it is your favorite.

2. To reflect on how your own attitudes toward writing have or have not changed as a result of writing about the reading in this chapter, try one of the following activities.

   • Complete in five different ways the sentence, "I used to think/feel/know _____ about writing, but now I think/feel know _____."

   • Write a poem about writing following this format: first line is an adjective; second line is two adverbs; third line is three verbs ending in -*ing*; fourth line is a prepositional phrase; fifth line starts with *that*, *which*, *because*, *since*, or *although*; sixth line is like the fourth line; seventh is like the third; eighth is like the second; and ninth is one adjective again.

   • Imagine that your students tell you they do not want to write and do not like to do so. Script out the explanation you might deliver to them that details why you use writing-to-learn strategies in your classroom and how the use of such strategies fits your definition of teaching and learning.

   • Write a letter to us, the authors, explaining what you found valuable about the chapter and what questions you have.

CLASSROOM CARRY-OVER

Here's how I plan to use what I just learned about writing in the interactive classroom.

_____

_____

_____

_____

_____

_____

_____

_____

_____

_____

_____

_____

_____

_____

_____

_____

_____

_____

_____

_____

_____

_____

_____

_____

_____

_____

_____

_____

_____

_____

_____

_____

_____

CHAPTER 7

Instruction Planners

In this text we describe the role of the learner as one of "constructor of knowledge." The role of the teacher is that of "facilitator and director" for students engaged in the act of constructing knowledge. For such construction to take place, students need to be in an environment that is interactive; they need to be in a place in which they can safely make the best use of their listening, speaking, reading, and writing skills as they interact with each other, the teacher, audiovisual materials, and course content to create new meaning.

As you develop your content-based lessons, use the following questions to remind you of essential guidelines for creating an interactive classroom environment.

WHEN MY STUDENTS ARE LISTENING IN THIS LESSON, HAVE I . . .

1. circumvented possible inhibitors to effective listening?

2. tapped prior experience by building on students' existing real-life experiential knowledge base, by asking students to brainstorm what they already know—or think they know—about a topic, or by helping students to generate questions they have about a topic based on their existing knowledge base?

3. provided a purpose for listening by giving instructions, by providing questions to be answered or a guide sheet to be completed during the listening, or by making a controversial or provocative statement?

4. paused in the midst of the provision of verbal material to ask questions that help students synthesize the material or reconnect the world of their experience with the new material?

5. guided reflection by using a reflective journal, by guiding note taking, or by choosing a class recorder?

6. considered using graphic organizers to help students process and organize material? (Venn diagrams, sequence chains, detail diagrams, structured webs, hypothesis-building charts, decision-making charts)

7. provided visual reinforcement for the verbal input?

8. modeled and encouraged active listening by paraphrasing the speaker, by collecting comments visually, and by using Dillon's seven active listening strategies?

WHEN MY STUDENTS ARE SPEAKING IN THIS LESSON, HAVE I . . .

1. provided an appropriate setting; that is, have I considered the room arrangement, the arrangement of the desks, and other environmental factors?

2. carefully considered group size and organization appropriate for my purpose and objectives?

3. made clear the purpose for speaking?

4. provided sufficient background of instruction to ensure success on the part of both speaker and listeners, especially in the case of oral reports and other "formal" speaking tasks?

5. provided sufficient time to prepare for students involved in speaking based on group work and independent research?

6. selected appropriate group activities, such as cooperative learning or think/pair/share options, to facilitate students' verbal interactions?

7. encouraged students to use graphic organizers to facilitate their audience's ability to understand?

8. modeled some effective speaking myself?

IF MY STUDENTS ARE READING IN THIS LESSON, HAVE I . . .

1. considered using a Directed Reading Activity, Directed Reading-Thinking Activity, or Directed Inquiry Activity format to help students process the reading?

2. included in the lesson an opportunity for students to tap their backgrounds about the reading topic?

3. planned how I will develop their background for the reading, if necessary?

4. planned to teach directly vocabulary words prerequisite to the understanding of the reading selection?

5. planned to have the students induce the definition of key vocabulary words through the vocabulary priming process?

6. ensured that the students will have an explicitly stated purpose for reading?

7. considered the use of graphic organizers to help students collect information for achieving their purpose for reading?

8. provided opportunities for the students to collaborate in order to facilitate the understanding of the reading?

COULD MY STUDENTS WRITE IN THIS LESSON IN ORDER TO . . .

1. tap their background of experience, either individually or collaboratively, or review their existing knowledge base?

2. apply knowledge as an expert in the field would do?

3. record observations and reflections for future use?

4. assess the gaps in their knowledge and develop their own questions to guide their learning?

5. generalize steps in a procedure, demonstrate understanding of key issues, or demonstrate comprehension of ideas by putting them into their own words?

6. make personal connections with new material and clarify their personal thoughts about and responses to material and class activities?

7. provide feedback to the teacher about what students did learn and what is still unclear after a lesson?

8. develop readiness for reading or for another sort of extension activity?

9. analyze their own progress and take responsibility for improving their performance based on that assessment?